GORGEOUS LEATHER CRAFTS

GORGEOUS LEATHER CRAFTS

30 Projects to Stamp, Stencil, Weave & Tool

Kari Lee

LARK BOOKS

A Division of Sterling Publishing Co., Inc.
New York

EDITOR:
Katherine Duncan Aimone

ART DIRECTOR:
Tom Metcalf

COVER DESIGN:
Barbara Zaretsky

PRODUCTION ASSISTANT:
Shannon Yokley

PHOTOGRAPHY:
Keith Wright
(www.keithwright.com)

ILLUSTRATIONS:
Orrin Lundgren

EDITORIAL ASSISTANCE:
Veronika Alice Gunter,
Rain Newcomb

*Many thanks from Lark
Books to Jeff Seitz, and
Sandi Bowman, both of
Asheville, North Carolina, for
opening their beautiful
homes to us to use as
locations for photography.*

Library of Congress Cataloging-in-Publication Data

Available

10 9 8 7 6 5 4 3 2 1

First Edition

Published by Lark Books, a division of

Sterling Publishing Co., Inc.

387 Park Avenue South, New York, N.Y. 10016

© 2002, Kari Lee

Distributed in Canada by Sterling Publishing, c/o Canadian Manda Group, One Atlantic Ave.,
Suite 105 Toronto, Ontario, Canada M6K 3E7

Distributed in the U.K. by Guild of Master Craftsman Publications Ltd., Castle Place,
166 High Street, Lewes, East Sussex, England BN7 1XU

Tel: (+ 44) 1273 477374, Fax: (+ 44) 1273 478606, Email: pubs@thegmcgroup.com,
Web: www.gmcpublications.com

Distributed in Australia by Capricorn Link (Australia) Pty Ltd.,

P.O. Box 704, Windsor, NSW 2756 Australia

If you have questions or comments about this book, please contact:
Lark Books
67 Broadway
Asheville, NC 28801
(828) 253-0467

Printed in Hong Kong

ISBN 1-57990-251-0

CONTENTS

office possibilities

dining room and table accents

elegant home accessories

wearable art

Introduction

As a project developer and designer I've had the opportunity to spend many hours experimenting with the vast number of products and tools available on the leather market as well as the wider crafts market. Through trial and error and the experiences of others, I've discovered what works and doesn't work. Through this book, I'm happy to share things that I've discovered and developed within the realm of this exciting and popular craft.

Once considered territory for hobbyists, leather craft has now been adopted by contemporary designers such as myself who are looking for new means of expression. Whether you are a beginner or a seasoned designer, this book will inspire and delight you. Written as a reference as well as a project book, it introduces you to the characteristics of various leathers as well as the basic tools and techniques of leather working. You'll be guided with tried-and-true construction techniques that leather workers have used for years. The large front section of the book will give you plenty of information before you undertake the projects that teach you more through detailed how-to photos.

Through the projects, you'll be presented with innovative and stylish approaches to an old and revered art. Your imagination will be ignited by the many looks and choices—from handsome home accessories to luxurious garments—that can be created from leather, suede, and rawhide. From traditional techniques such as tooling and branding, to today's surface design obsession with stamping and stenciling, you'll find the melding of old and new influences irresistible.

You'll discover that there are many ways to embellish or construct a project. (If you're rebellious and curious like I am, you may not want to always stick with the instructions! Experimenting is great, but always test out combinations of materials before undertaking a variation of a project.) With practice gained through this book, you'll become proficient and create a style of your own.

I hope you'll consider this book a ticket to have fun and explore the interesting possibilities for working with a material that will endure for years to come.

stamped along the edge of the back side of it. When buying leather, you'll also notice that it is graded to indicate its quality. Premier leather is graded as the best (or first).

Because leather is a natural material, it often has blemishes, holes, creases, or thinning areas on its surface. Some blemishes can add to the appearance of the finished piece. Before you make a piece, you should take these areas into consideration when selecting areas to cut out from patterns.

Some leathers are buffed by a machine to remove defects before being sold. If the leather is called *full* or *top grain*, this designation means that the leather hasn't been buffed. If you plan to dye the leather, full grain is preferable.

When you're selecting a leather or suede that has been dyed, use a white

Leather, Suede, and Rawhide

This section will introduce you to the characteristics of various types of leather and suede, including how it is graded, sold, and packaged.

Selecting and Purchasing Leathers or Suedes

In its raw form, leather varies in thickness. To create different thicknesses and weights for commercial use, the skin is run through a splitting machine with the grain (or right side up). The underside (or flesh side) that is sliced off results in what is called a *split*, which is used for making suede or

embossed leather. (Embossed leather is run through a press to create an overall decorative imprint on its surface.)

The thickness of the leather is measured in ounces. For instance, when you purchase what is known as vegetable-tanned leather (see page 9), it comes in a range from 1 to 5 ounces (.41 to 1.98 mm). When you're planning projects with suede or leather, the weight should always be considered.

Leather and suede is also sold by the square foot, and each skin or hide varies in size. The pelt of an animal smaller than a cow is referred to as a skin, and the pelts of larger animals are called hides. The size of each skin or hide is

Ounces	Irons	Fractional Inches	Decimal Inches	Metric
1 oz.	.75	1/64	0.016	0.41 mm
2 oz.	1.50	1/32	0.031	0.78 mm
3 oz.	2.25	3/64	0.047	1.19 mm
4 oz.	3.00	1/16	0.063	1.60 mm
5 oz.	3.75	5/64	0.078	1.98 mm
6 oz.	4.50	3/32	0.094	2.39 mm
7 oz.	5.25	7/64	0.109	2.78 mm
8 oz.	6.00	1/8	0.125	3.18 mm
9 oz.	6.75	9/64	0.141	3.58 mm
10 oz.	7.50	5/32	0.156	3.96 mm
11 oz.	8.25	11/64	0.172	4.37 mm
12 oz.	9.00	3/16	0.188	4.78 mm
13 oz.	9.75	13/64	0.203	5.17 mm
14 oz.	10.50	7/32	0.219	5.57 mm
15 oz.	11.25	15/64	0.234	5.95 mm

Chart converting ounces of leather or suede to other equivalents

cloth to rub the surface and find out if any color comes off easily. If so, you're observing what is known as *crocking*. You should avoid leathers that show signs of this condition, because the color can rub off onto adjoining leather or suede pieces or even your furniture.

You should also pay attention to the hand or the feel of the leather when buying it. (For example, you'll need a light, soft, and pliable suede for clothing or pillows and a much stiffer suede for making durable place mats or a desk pad.) As you study each of the projects in this book, you'll note the use of different weights and feels in leathers and suedes.

If you need more than one skin or hide for a project, you should buy them together for uniformity in color, hand, and grain. (Skins come from tanneries in bundles that are dyed in lots.) Doing this won't guarantee that all of the leather is exactly the same size or grade, since some tanneries mix the grades in a bundle, but the color will be consistent.

When you're ready to puchase leather or suede for a project of your own design, you'll need to calculate the square footage that you need to buy. (To make this process easy when you're learning, the projects in this book list the square footage that you need for each.)

If you're using a purchased pattern that provides you with the width and yardage of the fabric needed, use the chart on this page to convert the yardage into square footage. (If you're using suede, use the yardage listed on your pattern for napped fabric.)

After determining how much leather you'll need, add an extra 20 to 25 percent to account for irregularities in the shape of skins and hides and the possibility of surface imperfections.

If the average size of the leather or suede in a batch is not consistent, you should purchase an extra one to make certain that you won't come up short on the square footage.

Small pieces of vegetable-tanned leather and suede known as *trim pieces* are available in craft stores. When making small projects that don't demand large pieces of leather, you can purchase these swatches at an affordable price.

Commonly Used Leathers and Suedes

The following kinds of leather are some of the most commonly used. The average size and weight of the skin or hide is provided.

•*Vegetable-tanned leather:* This type of leather (most often cowhide) has been tanned with plant and wood materials. It is known for its blond, smooth, and absorbent surface that has a heavy, stiff hand. It works well for tooling and molding. Depending on the project, you can select a weight of this leather that ranges from 1 to 15 ounces (.41 to 5.95 mm). The size of each piece of leather will vary, depending on the cut of the hide.

A skin of vegetable-tanned leather that is a calf or kidskin is sold whole. The average square footage for a calf is 6 to 15 feet (1.8 to 4.5 m), with weights available from about 1 to 3 ounces (.41 to 1.19 mm). The average square footage for a kid is 3 to 5 feet (.9 to 1.5 m) and 1 to 2 ounces (.41 to .78 mm). Because a cowhide is large, it is sold as a side or shoulder. The best part of the hide is the butt, followed by the shoulder.

•*Deer-tanned cowhide:* This leather is tanned to be as soft and supple as deerskin (see next page), yet it has the durability of cowhide. It lacks the flexibility of deerskin, which is desirable for certain projects. It weighs 3 to 4 ounces (1.19 to 1.6 mm) and averages 18 to 22 square feet (1.6 to 2 m²), or about double the size of deerskin. Deer-tanned cowhide is offered in pre-dyed earth-tone colors.

36-inch (.9 m) width =
9 square feet (.81 m²)

45-inch (1.1 m) width =
11 square feet (1 m²)

54-inch (1.3 m) width =
13 square feet (1.2 m²)

60-inch (1.5 m) width =
15 square feet (1.4 m²)

•*Deerskin:* Deerskin or buckskin retains its grain surface after tanning and has a soft, pliable hand. It can be purchased in 2-to 3-ounce (.78 to .047 mm) garment weight and averages 9 square feet (.8 m²).

•*Kidskin:* This is a soft, pliable skin that works well for small projects. It averages 3 to 6 feet (.9 to 1.8 m) in size with a weight of 1 to 2 ounces (.41 to .78 mm).

•*Suede:* The term suede refers to the finish of the leather rather than to the skin or hide that is used. Suede is distinctive for its soft, textured surface. It is typically acquired from the flesh side (non-grain side) of the skin.

For projects that require a cost-conscious suede surface that is soft yet durable, you can use a 4-ounce (1.6 mm) cow suede. Available in bright colors, it works well for a variety of projects including purses and other wearable pieces.

A garment-weight cowhide suede, made from cowhide splits, weighs 2 to 3 ounces (.78 to 1.19 mm) and averages 10 to 12 square feet (.9 to 1 m²). This suede has an ultra-soft, pliable surface and is available in rich, warm colors. It works well for garments as well as larger projects such as home accessories.

Pig suede, more expensive than cow suede, is velvety soft with a supple hand. The selection of colors now available makes it increasingly desirable for garments and home decor. It is soft enough to sew on most home sewing machines. The average size is 12 square feet (1 m²) and weighs ½ to 2 ounces (.20 to .78 mm).

Metal stamps are used for tooling the surface of leather on a marble slab or solid punch board. A caddy is convenient for holding stamping tools as well as chisels and drive punches.

•*Rawhide:* This is a skin that has been cleaned and dehaired, but not tanned (as are soft, pliable leathers). After cleaning, it is dried, resulting in a stiff, ridged surface that has a rustic look. A rawhide side from a cow weighs 4 to 6 ounces (1.6 to 2.39 mm) and averages 6 square feet (.5 m²). A rawhide side weighs 4 to 6 ounces (1.6 to 2.39 mm) and averages 21 square feet (1.9 m²). Rawhide can also be puchased with natural (cream) or bleached white surface. Goatskin parchment is lighter. It averages ½ to 1 ounce (.20 to .41 mm) and 5 square feet (.45 m²).

Preparing Your Work Space

When working with leather, you'll need an organized space with adequate storage for materials, supplies, and tools. Keep tools on a shelf or table within arm's reach of your work surface. A caddy for holding stamps and punches is convenient. Extra leather can be rolled up or stored flat in a dark, dry place. The surface as well as your hands should be clean and free of all dirt and oil. Make sure that your space is well-ventilated—especially if you are using cements, solvents, or a wood-burning tool (for branding leather).

You'll spend much of your time standing or sitting at a worktable or other surface on which you cut, tool, brand, mold, stitch, or treat the leather in a number of ways. A sturdy wooden table at a comfortable height is recommended. A width of at least 4 feet (1.2 m) and a length of at least twice the width is ideal; this size allows you plenty of room to lay out patterns for cutting.

If you don't have a table that is this large, you can improvise by placing a large, sturdy 4 x 8-foot (1.2 x 2.4 m) piece of ½-inch (1.3 cm) foam board (available at office supply stores) on the floor for laying out patterns and cutting. When working on a table or the foam board, you must use a self-healing mat or a punch board on top of it to protect it from cut marks and give longer life to the blades of your knives.

When you punch holes or tool (leather), you'll need to work on a harder surface. For punching holes, you should place a solid punch board or a piece of dense, smooth wood on your work surface. For tooling (which includes stamping leather with metal tools pounded with a mallet), a marble slab is recommended. (To reduce the noise of pounding, place a thin towel between the leather and marble slab.)

To prepare your surface for applying stain, dye, or paint, cover it with a sheet of plastic or thick paper.

Basic Leather Tools

In the course of your work, you'll find that there are a few finishing tools for leather that you'll use over and over. (Other tools that you'll need are discussed throughout the rest of the book.) The following list gives you a brief introduction to tools created specifically for use with leather and suede that can be purchased at tack and leather stores or through leather suppliers.

• *Modeling tools:* These multi-purpose tools with two ends are used for many functions including tracing pattern lines, drawing the lines of designs, and sculpting or embossing designs on moist leather. The ends of them come in a variety of shapes.

• *Skiver:* This tool with replaceable, razor-like blades for paring (skiving) is used to reduce the thickness of leather along the edges. Always use it on the backside of the leather, not the front. Practice using the tool to gauge the angle and pressure that makes a smooth and uniform cut.

• *French edger:* This handled tool with an extended metal blade is used to create a flat-surfaced bevel along the edge of leather, gouge channels in leather, or reduce leather thickness by cutting away thin layers (skiving). The lower edge of the tool must be kept flat against the bottom edge of the leather and work surface with firm pressure when you're using it.

• *Edgers and edge bevelers:* These tools are used to trim off the corners along the edges of leather to create a

•Skiver

•Saftey skiver

•V-gouge

•Circle edge slicker

•Modeling tools

•French edger, edger and edge beveler

round edge. They are available in several sizes, and the one that you choose depends on the weight of the leather. The tip of the edger must be held at a 45° angle. A smooth, continuous thread of leather from the beveled edge indicates that you're using it properly.

• *Circle edge slicker:* Once the edge of the leather has been rounded with an edge beveler, you'll use this round tool with a slotted edge to burnish it and make it smooth. First, dampen the edge with a sponge and water. Hold the edge of the leather with a firm grip, and quickly rub the tool back and forth, working on a small section at a time.

• *V-gouge:* This tool with an adjustable blade to accommodate different leather thicknesses is used for gouging fold lines on the backside of leather. To cut a line, position a straightedge on the leather, and push the tool away from you with firm and controlled pressure to remove about half of the leather's thickness.

Cutting and Punching Leather and Suede

When you're ready to cut your leather or suede, always place the leather or suede grain side up on the cutting mat. Cut out your patterns from durable poster board to provide a clean edge to guide your knife. Always position the patterns on the leather skin or hide along the direction of the backbone of the skin from the head to the tail. (This will provide you with leather pieces that stretch less.) To keep patterns in place while you cut, weigh them down with sewing weights or bricks that you've wrapped in paper.

A variety of cutting tools: leather shears, craft knife, craftsman's knife with interchangeable blades ("clicker knife"), decorative-edged scissors, and rotary cutters

To cut out leather or suede pieces, you'll need a knife that is appropriate for the project as well as the size of your hand. Always use a sharp blade, and hold the knife firmly in an upright position while you cut towards yourself.

A craft knife is easy for small hands to grip and is preferred for cutting and trimming detail pieces when working with thin leather or suede. This kind of knife has replaceable blades, and there is no sharpening involved. A slightly larger all-purpose craftsman's knife (or "clicker" knife) with a wooden handle and separate straight and curved blades that can be sharpened is ideal for cutting leather. This kind of knife is available in tack, leather, and some craft and hobby stores and can be used to cut both thick and thin leathers. The straight blade works well for cutting a straight line or a broad curve. The curved blade will help you negotiate more detailed curves or edges.

To make a simple strop for sharpening blades, cut a long strip of vegetable-tanned leather or poster board. On the grain side of the leather or the mat side of the poster board, rub an even coat of white jeweler's rouge. Place

Using a strop to sharpen blades

the strop on your work surface, and use firm pressure to pull the blade of the knife toward you. Make sure that the blade's beveled edge is flush with the board.

If you prefer to use a pair of shears rather than a knife to cut leather or suede, make sure to buy the ones made for leather. Available in tack, leather, and some craft stores, their long handle and short blades with razor-sharp edges produce a powerful cutting action that will allow you to cut through the heaviest leathers.

Rotary cutters, available at sewing and craft stores, can also be used as an alternative to cut leather. Their large and easy-to-grip handles and round steel blades can cut through lighter-weight leather or suede that is 8 to 9 ounces (3.18 to 3.58 mm). Decorative-edged blades made for rotary cutters or decorative-edged scissors made for cutting heavy fabrics can be used to embellish the edges of leather pieces.

Punching Holes or Slits

Steel punches, made for punching holes in leather or suede, come in a variety of shapes and sizes. The holes can serve both functional and decorative purposes. (For instance, you might use punches to create holes for lacing or stitching or to make a perforated design on suede.) The most commonly used punches are round, oval, and oblong. Decorative punches such as stars, hearts, and diamonds are also available in several sizes.

The top half of a punch tool is solid, which allows you to strike it with a mallet without damaging it. The lower

A variety of cutting tools: chisels, punches, rotary punch, awl with interchangeable blades

half of the tool is a hollow shaft with a small opening on the very end that is tapered into various shapes. In the middle of the shaft is a small opening that allows an exit point for the punched leather.

Place a punch board on your work surface. Hold the punch perpendicular to the work surface before striking it sharply to drive the tapered steel shape through the leather.

Keep several things in mind when selecting a mallet. A wooden mallet is lightweight and great for getting started in leather craft. Polymer mallets are made to last—they perform with little bounce and won't damage the tools. Among leather crafters, the rawhide mallet is considered to be the best. Polymer and rawhide mallets are available in a variety of weights.

You can also punch holes with a rotary punch. This tool has a handle grip and a rotating wheel that holds up to six different round tubes of various sizes. Some come with extra tubes for replacing ones that wear out. To use this tool, turn the wheel until the desired tube size faces the metal punching pad on the opposite arm. Slide the leather between the tube and pad, and squeeze the handles together firmly to punch the hole.

Pronged chisels with one or more prongs are used to create slits for lacing or stitching leather or suede. A single-prong chisel can be used for making slits to attach hardware fasteners such as spots (see page 23). Chisel prongs range in size from 3/32-inch (2.4 mm) to 1/8-inch (3 mm). Multiple-prong chisels come with three, four, or eight prongs that are straight or angled. To punch slits, firmly hold the chisel perpendicular to the surface. Sharply strike the top of it with a mallet to drive the prongs through the leather.

Several types of awls are used to pierce holes in leather or suede. Awls are made with single blades attached to handles or as sets with interchange-able blades that screw in and out of handles. Among them, the scratch awl, with a sharp rounded blade, is used to pierce holes for saddle stitching (see page 21) or scratch pattern lines on the surface of the leather. A fid awl has a flat, blunt point that is used to enlarge the holes in leather for lacing thick lace or thread. Diamond-shaped awl blades are available for piercing holes for sewing.

Appling stain to vegetable-tanned leather

Marking a line with a scratch awl

Dyes, Stains, and Paints

In the development stage of your proj-ect, keep in mind what type of finish you plan to use for your leather or suede sur-face. These choices range from pene-trating dyes and stains to accents created with colorful paints. In general, you should always test dyes, stains, and paints on a swatch of the leather that you plan to use for a project.

Dyes and Stains

Dyes and stains, available in both sol-vent and water-based forms, penetrate the surface of leather. Stains, which are slightly thicker than dyes and tend to streak, are almost always used to lend an antique effect to leather. They highlight imperfections and the grain of the leather. Dyes, on the other hand, give full and even coverage.

Dyes and stains are used primarily on vegetable-tanned leather. (Suedes are already dyed.) Always apply dyes and stains to a larger surface than needed for the pieces that you plan to cut out, since the leather will shrink after it dries. To get even coverage on the sur-face of the leather, look for imperfec-tions before dyeing or staining, because these areas tend to absorb the dye more heavily.

The surface of leather must be clean for dyes and stains to penetrate it. To make a simple cleaning solution, mix 1 teaspoon (5 mL) of oaxic acid (avail-able at hardware stores) in a pint (.47 L) of water until the chemical is dissolved. Use a soft rag and the solu-tion to lightly and quickly wipe the sur-face clean, removing acidic residues.

After swabbing the surface, allow it to dry completely before dyeing it. If you don't want to mess with mixing a solution, commercial cleaners that do the same job are available through leather suppliers. (Caution: Be sure to store all such cleaning chemicals away from children.)

To get consistent coverage when dyeing or staining leather, apply several light coats of color as opposed to one heavy coat. Dyes and stains will be slightly altered by the inherent reddish-yellow color of vegetable-tanned leather. Over time, this leather, along with the applied color, will darken with age.

A permanent, alcohol-based dye called "spirit" dye is the one that is most often chosen by leather workers to create a black surface, because it deeply penetrates the surface. Available in other colors as well, it works best on vegetable-tanned leather. A solvent may be used to thin this dye to attain different values.

Water-based dyes are nonflammable and easy to clean up, but they don't penetrate the surface or appear as rich as spirit dyes. Nevertheless, you can get rich color by applying several coats, and they can be thinned with water to create different values.

Paints and Other Color Options

Today, crafters and artists experiment with all kinds of craft and art media that are not made specifically for leather, but can be used successfully. Be sure to test them out on a scrap of leather or suede before using them.

•*Water-based acrylic paints:* These are the paints of choice for detail work on leather. Bright and opaque, they can be applied in one coat when used full strength. To make sure that any paint

Applying paint to a branded design

you use is right for your surface, test it out to make sure that it is soft and flexible after it dries.

If the paint isn't flexible after drying, you can add water to the paint beforehand so that some saturation occurs. A better alternative is to add a medium such as fabric medium to the paint so that it will penetrate the surface more and be flexible.

•*Fabric paint:* If you use good fabric paints on leather, they will be easily absorbed into the surface and will remain soft and flexible after drying. Most fabric paints require heat setting, but this isn't necessary if they are used on rawhide or vegetable-tanned leather. Instead, seal the surface with two light coats of spray acrylic leather finish to give it a flexible, durable, water-repellent finish.

•*Stencil paint:* This paint is thick and comes in vibrant colors that last. A dry-brush technique works the best for stenciling. A special round brush with a blunt end is made for stenciling on the paint. Load it with a light but even amount of paint before pouncing and swirling it into the open areas of the stencil.

•*Edge coat:* For finishing the edges of cut leather pieces, you can use acrylic-based edge coat, which is specially formulated for this purpose.

•*Stamp pads:* Permanent, dye-based stamp pads or fabric inks give the best results for applying color with stamps on leather or suede. There are also new brands of pigment inks on the market that dry quickly (unlike regular pigment inks), which can work well for stamping on leather or suede.

•*Markers:* Fabric, paint, and watercolor markers can be used on leather and deerskin. Fabric markers work well but will streak if attempting to color large areas. Water-based (not solvent-based) paint markers are recommended for use only on leather. Watercolor markers can be blended on the surface and won't bleed if you spray the colored area with a coat of acrylic leather finish. (With time, watercolor markers will fade somewhat.)

Finishes and Sealers

Whether you want to polish the surface of your leather with wax to give it a soft, mellow finish, or protect a painted surface with a coat of spray finish, there are several options for finishing and sealing. The finishes and sealers discussed below are for use on leather only. (A protective spray for suede is available in shoe and shoe repair stores.)

•*Leather wax:* This neutral-colored wax is applied with a soft cloth to soften and polish the leather surface.

•*Stain wax:* This colored wax serves the purpose of staining as well as waterproofing and finishing leather.

•*Spray acrylic leather finish:* A coat of this clear finish adds a tough, durable, water-repellent finish to leather and is glossy after it dries.

•*Natural highlighter:* Like a stain, this natural-colored medium darkens the leather slightly while accentuating carving, tooling, and flaws on the leather's surface. Additional applications may be applied for a darker shade.

Applicators

The following section will tell you the best ways to apply dyes, stains, paints and other color options, finishes, and sealers. The tools used are simple, but you should test each out on a scrap of leather to get a feel for them.

•*Sponge:* You'll need a clean sponge to apply water to the surface of the leather (casing). It can also be used for applying dye to edges and for dyeing the overall surface.

•*Wool:* Soft scraps of sheep's wool are used to apply stain to leather. Wash and dry the scraps first to remove any loose fibers before staining. Then apply a liberal amount of stain to the wool, working it quickly and evenly across the leather surface. To remove any excess stain, use a soft, water-moistened cloth to rub the surface with a circular motion.

•*Paintbrushes:* There are numerous shapes and sizes of artist's paintbrushes on the market that can be adapted for applying dyes or paints. Experiment with brushes to find out what works for you. The following descriptions will give you a few tips:

A variety of applicators: stenciling brushes, sponge, strips of cardboard, foam brayer, craft syringe, foam-tip brushes, paintbrushes

◊ A flat, sable brush works well for applying dye to large surface areas. To get even coverage, slightly overlap strokes in one direction before painting back over them diagonally. Continue this process until you're satisfied with the coverage.

◊ To achieve a diluted, washed effect with dyes, use a brush made of squirrel hair. Work quickly, using a circular motion to creat overlapping strokes.

◊ A sable or synthetic sable brush should be used for painted detail and decorative work.

•*Cosmetic sponge:* A wedge-shaped cosmetic sponge works well for applying a light, even coat of paint to the face of a rubber stamp.

•*Foam-tip brush:* This brush with an angled cut works well for coating the cut edges of leather with dye or paint.

•*Brayer:* For even coverage and a resulting sharp image, use a foam brayer to apply paint or dye from a stamp pad or bottle onto rubber stamps. Brayers can also be used to cover leather surfaces with paint or dye.

•*Craft syringes:* When a detailed application of dye, paint, or adhesive is required, there is no better tool to use than a syringe. The thickness of the liquid that you're using will determine the style that you choose.

Laces, Threads, and Needles

Laces, threads, and needles are used for both assembly and embellishment of leather and suede. The following section will give you an overview of these materials and tools.

Laces

Because lacing can be used to secure layers of leather or purely as embellishment, you should consider strength as well as style when selecting a lace for your project. Holes that match the size of the lace must be punched in the leather or suede before lacing it (see pages 12 and 13).

The length of lace that you'll need for a project depends on the stitch that you're using (see page 21). For example, a running stitch requires approximately one and a half times the length of the edge or other feature that you're stitching, and a single whipstitch requires approximately three and a half times the length of the edge or other feature. If you're lacing heavy materials, they may require more length than the estimated length suggested here.

Below are some commonly used laces for leather:

•*Suede lace:* A decorative lace that is available in ⅛-inch (3 mm) and ⁵⁄₃₂-inch (4 mm) widths, this lace comes in a variety of colors that makes it versatile enough for a wide variety of projects. It is economical and colorful. Although it is cut from 4 to 6-ounce (1.6 to 2.39 mm) weight hides, it is not recommended when you need a strong lace.

An assortment of laces and thread with beeswax, needles, and thimbles

•*Latigo lace:* This very strong, durable lace is made from a heavy, oil-soaked leather that lends a rustic, outdoor look to projects. It is sold in ⅛-inch (3 mm) widths and is cut from 4 to 6-ounce (1.6 to 2.39 mm) leather.

•*Full-grain leather lace:* This is the ultimate in fine leather lace with an elegant and completely uniform shape that lies flat on a surface when you use it for stitching. This durable lace available in natural earth tones should be used for projects that you want to last. It is available in ⁵⁄₃₂-inch (2.4 mm) and ⅛-inch (3 mm) widths.

•*Bonded leather lace:* This lace made from bonded leather fibers is a less

expensive alternative to full-grain leather lace. It is a very strong, versatile, and uniform lace. It comes in ⁵⁄₃₂-inch (2.4 mm), ⅛-inch (3 mm), and ⁵⁄₃₂-inch (4 mm) widths.

•*Vinyl lace:* This inexpensive faux leather lace with beveled edges comes in plain and grained finishes. A reinforced core gives it strength. It is available in a wide variety of colors and is made in ⁵⁄₃₂-inch (2.4 mm) width only. It is appropriate for beginner projects or learning how to stitch.

•*Round lace:* This unique leather lace is cut from the center of the hide with a round bevel to make it uniform. Sold in 1 and 2 mm widths, it works well for embellishment purposes, such as adding beads to projects.

• *Braided cord:* This material is a very strong, economical alternative to round lace. To keep the cut ends from fraying, apply leather adhesive to them or burn them with a cigarette lighter.

Threads

The following threads are durable enough for assembling layers of leather by hand or machine and work well for decorative stitches. All are available at sewing or leather stores. (Caution: Never use 100 percent cotton thread with chemically tanned leather or suede because it will deteriorate.)

To begin hand stitching, you'll need to first calculate the thread length that you need. A rule of thumb to follow is to multiply the overall distance to be covered by four. To prepare your thread for hand stitching, apply a coat of beeswax by pulling the length of the thread across the block of wax until it is completely coated. To harden and burnish the wax, rub a piece of brown paper back and forth vigorously over the waxed thread. This step will keep your thread from fraying and knotting while stitching.

You can also purchase prewaxed threads to use for hand stitching that are available in bobbins or spools. Some are polyester, while others are a nylon and linen mix.

The following threads are recommended for leather working:

• *Linen:* Because of its strength, this sewing thread is perfect for hand stitching leather. It is available at tack and leather stores as well as craft stores, and comes prewaxed and ready for stitching.

• *Silk:* Silk thread has elasticity and tensile strength needed for both hand and machine stitching on leather or suede.

• *Polyester:* Polyester thread works well with leather and suede because it is strong and has the ability to stretch. Cotton-wrapped polyester thread works especially well. (The stretch of polyester thread may cause problems with the tension of your sewing machine, so make adjustments as needed.)

• *Nylon:* Twisted or bonded nylon thread is preferred for leather work, since a single strand tends to tear the leather or suede surface. It has a tendency to fray and generate static electricity when used in a sewing machine, so it is only recommended for hand stitching.

Lacing Needles

The two lacing needles listed below were developed for use with leather and suede laces. They provide the stability needed for lacing through prepunched holes and slits, making lacing much easier.

• *Two-prong lacing needle:* This needle is intended for use with $3/32$- to $5/32$-inch-wide (2.4 to 4 mm) flat, top-grain lace in prepunched holes that match the diameter of the lace. The lace length must be skived and tapered on the end before it is inserted between the needle's two layers of crafted steel. A tap from a mallet secures the lace.

• *Threaded lacing needle:* This needle was designed for lace widths from $3/32$- to $1/4$-inch (2.4 to 6 mm) and prepunched holes that match the diameter of the lace. Two sizes are available: one to accommodate $3/32$ to $1/8$-inch (2.4 to 3 mm) lace widths and a larger size for $1/8$ to $1/4$-inch (3 to 6 mm) lace. The skived and tapered end of the lace is inserted into the threaded cavity of the needle before the needle is rotated clockwise around the end of lace to attach it.

Needles Used for Hand Stitching Leather or Suede with Thread

Sewing needles can be adapted for sewing leather, and for other purposes, special leather needles are needed. Various needles are used in leather working to stitch through prepunched holes or directly through leather or suede.

The following two needles are most commonly used to sew or assemble leather or suede through prepunched holes:

• *Harness needle:* This round needle with a blunt end and a small eye for accomodating thin threads is used to stitch with ease through prepunched holes.

• *Big eye needle:* This needle with a blunt end and an extra large eye accommodates heavy threads for stitching through prepunched holes.

Because leather and suede are not easily penetrated with regular sewing needles, special needles are used to stitch directly on leather or suede by hand. The size of the needle that you use is related to the thickness of the leather or suede. When selecting a needle size for your project, you should keep in mind that a hole will remain where each stitch is made, which can weaken the stability of the skin or hide. For this reason, keep the size of the needle as small as possible for your purposes, and leave a reasonable amount of space between stitches.

The following are some of the needles most commonly used to stitch leather by hand with thread:

• *Glover's needle:* This needle that comes in a range of sizes has a triangular point which passes easily through leather and suede.

• *Sharp needle:* This strong needle with a small round eye works well for beading on leather or suede. Sharps are available in different sizes to accommodate the size of your beads.

Needles for Machine Sewing

Always consult your home sewing machine's manual for the suggested type and brand of needles to buy and use for leather or suede. While some universal and denim needles work fine for lightweight to medium-weight skins, using a leather needle of the right size is better if you have the option. A size 14 leather needle works well for machine sewing lightweight leather or suede, a size 16 for medium-weight, and a size 18 for heavyweight. Prior to machine sewing leather or suede for a project, test out the needle you plan to use on a scrap of the leather or suede to find a combination that works well without damaging the project materials. You must use a new needle for every project, no matter what needle you select.

Rubber cement and binder clips for basting

Assembly Materials and Methods

The following overview of simple assembly materials and methods will provide you with information that will help you as you undertake the projects in this book.

Using Adhesives

Adhesives are used in leather working for a variety of purposes including basting and binding seams. There are several brands of leather adhesive available on the market. Before you begin a project, read the manufacturer's instructions carefully, and test out each on a swatch of leather or suede.

When you adhere layers to one another, it's a good idea to place weights on top of each area as it dries. Bricks

wrapped in clean, heavyweight paper work well for this purpose.

(Caution: Some adhesives claim that they are permanent and can be dry-cleaned, but they don't always stand up to the process. For this reason, sewing is the best method of assembling any project that will need to be dry-cleaned.)

The following are the most commonly used adhesives for leather:

• *White leather adhesive:* This adhesive dries clear and flexible. It provides a strong bond that works well for gluing thin to medium-weight leather or suede. For the purposes of bonding, this adhesive is advised for those who may have health concerns about fumes resulting from solvent-based adhesives. Apply this adhesive to both surfaces, position them together while the adhesive is still wet, and apply pressure until they bond and dry.

•*Rubber cement:* This common adhesive can be used for temporarily tacking down or basting leather before it is stitched. It is most effective if you apply it to both surfaces and allow it to dry slightly before pressing the pieces together. It holds the leather firm, but the pieces can still be taken apart for adjustment. *(Health caution: Always use in a well-ventilated room or outdoors.)*

•*Contact cement:* Use contact cement if you need a permanent yet flexible adhesive. Like rubber cement, you should apply it to both surfaces and allow it to dry slightly before pressing the pieces together. It dries very quickly and has a permanent hold. *(Health caution: Always use in a well-ventilated room or outdoors.)*

Basting

Several simple notions can be used to temporarily secure leather or suede before it is hand or machine stitched:

•*Straight pins:* These simple sewing pins can be used if they are placed outside of the seam allowance where puncture marks don't matter.

•*Binder clips:* These office supply clips that come in a variety of sizes work very well to clamp leather or suede pieces together while you stitch them or to hold them as glues dry. To prevent damage to the leather or suede, glue small pieces of soft leather to the inside and outer edges of the clips.

Using binder clips to hold suede strips in place while weaving

•*Paper clips:* This office supply staple works to hold lightweight suede pieces together along the edges while sewing.

•*Clothespins:* Unsoiled clothespins work well for temporarily holding together pieces of rawhide.

•*Rubber cement:* As discussed in the previous section on gluing, a light application of rubber cement can be used to temporarily baste leather or suede pieces before stitching them. Make sure that you don't use the cement outside of the seam allowance, or it may show on the finished project. (If you plan to baste with rubber cement and then use a sewing machine, be extra careful to keep the cement away from the seam line, or your needle will get gummy.)

Hand Lacing and Stitching

Hand lacing on leather is a form of assembly that requires precisely punched holes or slits in the leather or suede and different types of needles (see page 19), depending on the width and thickness of the lace or thread being used. Both lacing and stitching can be functional (for assembly purposes) and/or decorative.

The following stitches are most commonly used in leather or suede assembly with either laces or threads:

•*Whipstitch:* This common sewing stitch used with both lace and thread can be used to permanently lace pieces together by hand through slits or holes that have been prepunched along the edges.

Lacing up a pillow sleeve by hand

• *Running stitch:* This basic sewing stitch that is usually done with thread is used for basting or securing leather seams through prepunched holes. The needle and thread are pushed in and out from the back to the front of the seam, leaving even, open spaces between the stitches. (This stitch is also known as a basting stitch.)

• *Saddle stitch:* A saddle stitch, done by hand with a single length of thread and a needle on both ends of the thread, looks like a double running stitch but is done differently when lacing two layers of leather together. To use this stitch, two pieces of leather are clamped in a *stitching and lacing pony* (also known as a clam)—a wooden stand shaped like an upside-

A stitching and lacing pony

down "T" that holds the leather firmly in place while you use both hands.

With the position of the holes for lacing premarked, you'll use a scratch awl to stab a hole through both layers of leather before you begin lacing. Two needles are used to stitch with one length of lace.

Sewing Leather or Suede with a Domestic Sewing Machine

Sewing leather and suede on a machine is no more difficult than sewing fabric, but it requires more time and planning. If you haven't sewn leather or suede on your machine before, take the time to read the manufacturer's handbook for recommended settings and accessories.

In preparation for sewing, attach the walking foot to your machine, followed by the recommended needle. After threading the machine, sew a test piece to experiment with settings and stitches on the leather or suede that you're using. As a general rule of thumb for most leather and suede, use eight to 10 stitches per inch (2.5 cm). (Never make the length of the stitches smaller than this, or the leather may tear.)

When you're sewing leather or suede, you should reduce the speed of the stitch because you're sewing through materials that are heavier than fabrics. By stitching slowly, you'll allow the machine to properly complete the stitch and avoid costly mistakes.

To prevent garment-weight suede from stretching when you sew it, first place ¾-inch (1.9 cm) strips of fusible interfacing (cut in the direction that has the

least amount of stretch) along the edges that you plan to sew. Follow the manufacturer's instructions for adhering the interfacing, and test it on a scrap of the suede that you'll be using for the project. (To protect the suede, place a cloth or pillowcase between the iron and the suede.)

To sew a plain seam with your machine, guide the leather or suede carefully, being careful not to pull or stretch it. Tie off the thread ends with square knots at the beginning and end of each seam.

Once a plain seam has been sewn, you can reduce the bulk of the leather or suede by trimming the seam with leather shears or a skiver. Press the seam open with your fingers and apply rubber cement to the back edges of it. Then use a roller tool or metal brayer to press open the seam allowance. Apply pressure while rolling the tool to smooth the seams flat.

If you press out a leather or suede seam with an iron, the iron should be set on a low to medium setting with no steam. Place a piece of heavy brown paper on top of the surface to be pressed so that the iron doesn't touch the leather or suede directly.

Finishing Seams with Special Stitches

There are several attractive ways of finishing sewn seams that can be applied to leather or suede.

To add double topstitching to a plain seam, press open the seam with a roller. (If you want, you can secure it by lightly basting it with rubber cement.) Sew two lines of stitching on top that are spaced ⅛-inch (3 mm) from the pressed seam on either side. Tie off the ends with square knots.

A mock flat-fell seam produces a neatly finished look. To sew this seam, place the grain side of the leather or suede pieces together before sewing the pieces with a plain seam. Press the seam allowance to one side, and place the piece faceup underneath the foot of your machine before topstitching a seam ¼-inch (6 mm) from the seam line through the three layers.

If you're using a lightweight fabric, such as silk, as a lining for suede or leather, you can use a French seam to finish the cut edges of the fabric. With the wrong sides of the fabric together, stitch a ¼-inch (6 mm) seam. Trim the seam to ⅛ inch (3 mm) before pressing it open. Position the right sides of the fabric together (enclosing the cut edges of the seam), and stitch ¼ inch (6 mm) from the previously stitched seam. Press the seam to one side.

Upholstering

Adding leather or suede upholstery to a simple piece of furniture is not as difficult as you might think. The wood or cushion to be upholstered is first covered with a piece of batting that is stretched and stapled into place. The leather is stretched and gathered to fit snugly over the edges of the batting before being stapled.

An electric staple gun is recommended for upholstering with leather or suede. (Read the manufacturer's booklet for a recommendation of the type of staple to use.)

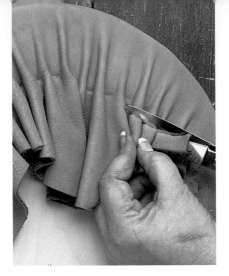

Trimming away the excess leather during upholstering

If you're planning to upholster a great number of your pieces, you should consider purchasing a pneumatic stapler and air compressor which works easily and efficiently to firmly position staples.

Embellishments and Hardware

To add dimension to your leather or suede projects, you can decorate the surface with both functional and decorative embellishments that range from upholstery tacks and grommets to beads and fringes. The following section introduces you to some of the options available, along with the tools that you'll need to add them to your projects:

• *Upholstery tacks:* These tacks with a single point attached to them were developed to secure leather or fabric to furniture. Today, they can be used for functional or purely decorative purposes. A wide range of designs, sizes, and finishes are available.

Tools and supplies for adding both functional and decorative embellishments: anvil and anvil strip with rivets, mallet, tack hammer, needle-nose pliers and upholstery tacks, base with setter tool and grommets, handled grommet setter, and fringes

To secure a tack to wood that is upholstered with leather or suede, hold the tack in a vertical position with a pair of needle-nose pliers before tapping it into place with a tack hammer. You can also use a rubber mallet for tacks that are spaced apart, but a tack hammer works better for tight areas.

• *Spots:* Spots are small pieces of hardware that are used to adorn leather or suede surfaces. They have a varying number of prongs and come in a variety of designs, sizes, and finishes.

To attach a spot, position it and mark its place by pressing the prongs onto the leather or suede until impressions remain to guide you. On top of a punch board, make small incisions with a $3/32$-inch (2.4 mm) single-prong lacing chisel and mallet before pushing the prongs through the leather or suede. Flip the piece over, and use the end of the chisel to fold the prongs down toward the center of the spot.

• *Rivets:* Rivets are small fasteners used to secure layers of leather together. They come in various dimensions, metals, and finishes, adding a decorative finish to projects. They are composed of two parts, often with a domed cap and a flat cap that are hammered together (the flat cap is placed on the backside of the leather or suede). Double-cap rivets have two caps that provide a finished look on both sides of the leather or suede.

To set rivets, you can use a small anvil made of cast iron, a mallet, and a rivet setter. Two types of anvils fit the needs of different caps: The upright anvil made for jewelry has a flat surface that works with a flat-headed cap, and a flat-strip anvil with a concave surface works well for domed caps.

The simplest rivet setter is made up of a metal shank that is concave on one end and flat on the other. The concave end fits over and preserves the domed cap of the rivet when its narrower shank is hammered into the wider shank of the flat-ended cap. During hammering, the narrow shank expands in the wider one to hold it in place.

To attach a rivet, use a punch that is the same diameter as the post of the rivet to punch a hole through the layers of material to be secured. Thread the shank of the rivet through the hole in the leather or suede. Place the upright jewelry anvil on your work surface. Position the flat-headed base of the rivet followed by the leather in the center of the anvil. Position the domed-headed part of the rivet over the flat-headed portion. Place the concave end of the rivet setter on the cap. Strike the other end of the rivet setter with the mallet, forcing the rivet post to expand.

To secure a double-cap rivet, use the flat-strip concave anvil. Position the bottom cap and leather on the anvil, and position the top cap over it. Hammer and set the cap with the mallet as described above.

• *Grommets:* A grommet is a round, two-part, reinforced eyelet that prevents leather or suede from tearing when a fastener or lace is passed through the opening in its center.

You can use a couple of different kinds of grommet setters. The first and less expensive is composed of a base with a setter tool. First, you must prepunch holes in the leather or suede where you plan to place the grommets with a

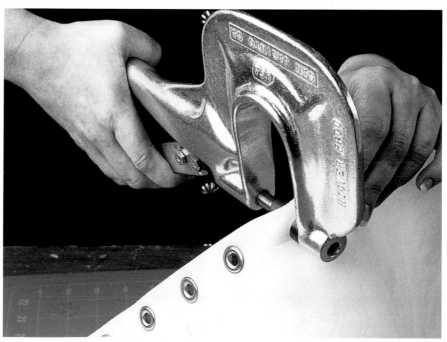

Securing grommets to rawhide with a handled grommet setter

PHOTO 1

PHOTO 2

punch that matches the grommet's size. On top of the base, place the top part of the grommet in the hole on the face of the leather or suede, and position the washer behind it on the other side of the material. Hold the setter tool firmly, and center it over the grommet before hammering it with the mallet to turn the edges of the top part of the grommet over the washer.

A second style of grommet setter resembles pliers and consists of steel handles with interchangeable parts for punching holes and setting different sized grommets. (The hole punch attachments work for thin suede, but aren't recommended for thicker leathers or suedes.) To set the grommets between the jaws of the tool, you must squeeze the handles together firmly.

• *Trims and fringe:* Trims and fringe made of various materials (including suede) can be used to embellish leather or suede projects. Hand or machine stitching is the best option for permanently securing trim or fringe to leather or suede.

You can also custom-make your own leather or suede fringe, which allows you to select the color, finish, and size that you prefer. To make your own fringe, use a knife or leather shears to cut a piece of leather or suede to the width and length of your choice (adding a margin to the width of the piece to serve as uncut top of the fringe). Use a stylus tool and a ruler to lightly mark a guideline that is about 3/8-inch (9.5 mm) from the top edge on the grain side of the leather or suede. Use a craft knife to cut fringe strands (1/8-inch [3 mm] strands are typical) perpendicular to the guideline (photo 1).

If you want to make twisted fringe, use deerskin or deer-tanned cowhide. After you've cut the fringe, secure the top edge of it with pushpins to a piece of mat board. Use a small spray bottle filled with water to lightly mist the fringe. Twist and pull each strand taut before releasing it (photo 2). Allow the twisted fringe to dry completely.

• *Leather lace and thongs:* You can cut a leather lace or thong in any width or length from any type of leather, suede, or rawhide for the purpose of lacing. To begin, cut out a circle from the material that you plan to use. The size of the circle will depend on the width and length of lace required for the project. (To estimate the size of the circle, you can cut out a mock circle from paper, then use scissors to cut the shape into a continuous strip of the width that you want, following a spiral pattern.)

After determining the size of the circle needed, cut it out with a craft knife or leather shears. Beginning at any point on the outer edge, cut out a continuous strip in a width of your choice from the circle.

•*Beads:* The vast selection of beads that are available to buy can add an elegant and exotic touch to leather or suede.

To attach beads to the surface of leather or suede, cut a length of evenly waxed thread or nylon bead cord no longer than an arm's length to prevent knotting and tangling. Choose a sharp or glover's needle that will fit through the hole of the beads you plan to use that is thick enough to pierce the leather or suede. For beading on medium (5 ounce [1.98 mm]) to heavy (9 to 10 ounce [3.58 to 3.96 mm]) leathers or suedes, you should pierce the needle through the top layer only, not all the way through the material. If you're working with a very stiff leather, you should prepunch holes through the leather before threading the beads onto the surface. Once the beading has

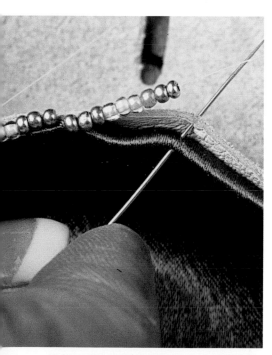

Using a sharp needle to secure beads to the edge of suede that is backed with silk

PHOTO **3**

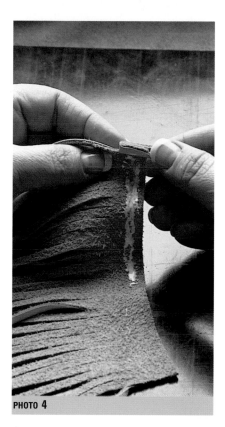

PHOTO **4**

been completed, secure the loose ends with several overhand knots.

•*Buttons:* Buttons, used as closures, come in many styles, sizes, and colors. To prevent the leather or suede from tearing due to use, use a glover's needle and waxed thread to sew a small button or stay on the reverse side of the leather or suede for reinforcement.

•*Tassels:* You can make your own tassels with precut or hand-cut fringe from leather or suede in a color of your choice. Keep in mind that the hand of the material will play a role in the finished look of the tassels.

To make tassels, use precut or hand-cut fringe of the length and width desired. With the grain side up, hold one side of the fringe with one hand, and with the other, pull the last strand of the fringe on the other side back and up to the top of the fringe to create a loop that is about an inch (2.5 cm) wide (photo 3). Use a dab of water-based leather glue or contact cement to secure the strand to the top margin of the fringe.

Apply a small amount of cement along the top edge of the flesh side of the fringe trim. Tightly roll the fringe trim grain side out around the bottom of the loop (photo 4).

Leather Working and Surface Decoration Techniques

Several basic techniques were selected for use in the projects that follow this section. They are described briefly below, along with the tools and some tips that are helpful when doing them. (You'll learn more about each technique as you undertake the projects.)

Weaving

Weaving with leather, suede, or rawhide produces an attractive and durable surface. You can create any number of patterns by varying the color and order of the strips in your weavings.

Weaving a chair bottom with painted leather strips

To weave the seat of a piece of furniture, you'll need a staple gun to attach the strips as you weave them. To assemble a woven covering over a pillow or other item, you can secure the edges with double-cap rivets. You can

Metal stamps and a swivel knife for tooling (see next page)

also lace or stitch the edges together through prepunched holes, or sew the edges together with a properly equipped sewing machine.

Molding

Molding leather involves thoroughly wetting vegetable-tanned leather and allowing it to dry slightly before pressing it into a mold of some sort to shape it. Once the leather dries, it retains the shape of the mold. Items such as bowls, masks, and handbags can be made with this technique.

Using a bowl to mold leather

First select a mold—a form made out of wood, thick ceramic, or plastic. Never use metal because it will stain the leather. Begin molding in shallow bowls to learn the technique. Whatever form you use, you'll have to eventually remove the dried leather from the mold and use it as it is (such as a bowl), or secure it back together with adhesive or lacing (such as a vase).

Selecting a weight of leather for a project can take some trial and error. When learning about molding leather, it's a good idea to purchase some inexpensive trim pieces with which to experiment. For instance, if the leather is too thick or thin, it may buckle. Lightweight leather may not hold the shape as well as the heavier weight leather does once it dries.

Tooling the leather surface

Tooling

Tooling is the process of decorating the surface of leather by carving and stamping with hand tools, most often on the surface of vegetable-tanned leather. Tooling requires patience and practice in order to master properly wetting the surface before tooling it (called "casing"), carving the leather, and gauging the right pressure to use for stamping impressions. After the tooling is completed, you can add color and finishes to enhance the design. Experiment with tooling on scrap pieces of leather to get a feel for it before moving on to finished projects.

• A *swivel knife* with an arched yoke at the top that holds a beveled blade can be used to cut or carve the outline of a design in leather before stamping it. A variety of swivel knives and interchangeable blades are available on the market. You can cut straight lines by using a straightedge along with the knife. To hold this knife properly, place your index finger in front of the first joint on the arched yoke at the top of the tool. Position the two middle fingers and your thumb along the shank of the tool. Center the blade (not leaning left or right), and lean the tool forward slightly before pulling it toward you in a straight or curved line. (You can make curved lines by rotating the barrel of the knife with your second and third finger and thumb.)

Always keep the side of your hand in contact with the leather surface to provide support while you cut. Control the pressure of the knife, and keep it from leaning to one side or another. The blade should cut through about half of the depth of the thickness of the leather.

In conjunction with swivel knives, steel stamping tools are used to create decorative impressions and patterns on leather as a part of tooling. Before beginning, place the cased leather faceup on a marble slab. With three fingers and your thumb, hold the tool perpendicular to the surface with your wrist and elbow firmly on the table. Strike the top of the tool once with the mallet, with force. (Use a mallet that is a comfortable weight for you. Never use a steel hammer with stamping tools.) Stamping a full, sharp impression will come with practice.

For some designs, you may want to make a partial instead of a full impression with one of the tools. To do this, tilt the tool slightly in the direction of the portion of the stamp that you want to impress before striking it.

Lots of stamping tools are available on the market that make a variety of impressions. Some of the more common stamping tools for leather are described below.

• *Bevelers* are used to cut lines that slant on one side at a 45° angle, lending the area inside the line a raised appearance. The angled head of this tool can be smooth or textured. Stamping with this tool requires a technique known as "walking." To do this, cut a beveled line with a swivel knife before placing the lowest edge of the tool toward you in the line. With a rapid and consistent movement, strike the top of the tool with the mallet, and inch the tool over slightly before striking it again. As you continue walking, you'll create a smooth, connected line.

• *Geometric tools* in various sizes and designs can be used to create overall, repeating patterns.

• *Veiners* have a half-moon shape, and are often used to simulate the veins of leaves or create background effects in a design.

• *Seeders* are round and come in a range of sizes and textures. They are often used to stamp the center of flowers or to add accents to border designs.

• *Camouflage tools* leave an impression made of vertical lines that resemble a clam shell. The base of this tool is shaped like a half moon, and the heel of the stamp is sloped, which causes it to make a deeper impression than the top of the stamp. This tool is often used to stamp flower petals and borders.

• *Shader tools* have pear-shaped ends that are rounded with no edges. They are used to create smooth textured areas within another carved area.

• *Pictorial tools* leave impressions of three-dimensional images of subjects such as animals or flowers.

• *Background tools* are used to create a stippled surface around the main stamped design to create depth and set off the main image.

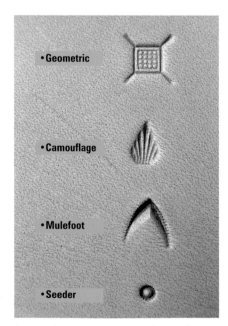

Impressions made by stamping tools

Branding

Branding the surface of leather with a hot iron to create designs is one of the most traditional forms of leather working. To brand leather today, you can use a common woodburning tool available at craft stores. This tool that is made to be held like a large marker, has interchangeable tips that can be used to draw lines and designs on leather. Tips with specific shapes can be used to stamp simple border designs or patterns.

Branding the surface of leather with a woodburning tool

Pieces of suede basted in place with rubber cement in preparation for appliquéing

Photo Transfers

Transferring photos or other images to leather or rawhide can provide you with limitless ways of altering and decorating the surfaces of your projects.

A family photo transferred to leather

Appliqué

Suede or leather appliqué can add a rich decorative touch to any garment, fashion accessory, or home décor item. And you don't have to make a large investment in materials to do it, because garment or lightweight suede can be purchased in a package that holds a mixture of trim pieces in different sizes and colors.

Leather shears can be used to cut effortlessly through garment-weight suede appliqué pieces, and you can use a rotary cutter or decorative-edged shears to cut heavier leather or suede. To make sewing easier, baste the pieces in place with a light application of rubber cement before you hand or machine stitch them. Avoid putting rubber cement close to the seam allowance.

Perforating

Leather and suede surfaces (especially on garments) are often decorated with perforated designs. Along with round and oblong punches, decorative shapes can be used to make patterns. A wonderful effect can be created by layering a perforated design in one color of leather or suede on top of a contrasting color.

Punches and a mallet are used to perforate a pattern on suede

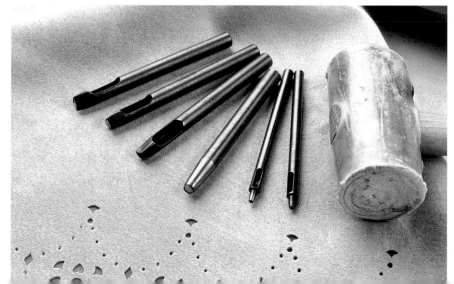

Iron-on Transfers

To make black-and-white or color iron-on transfers on leather, you can buy transfer paper for use with photocopiers at a copy center, or print onto transfer paper purchased at an office supply store made for use with an ink jet or a laser printer. Vegetable-tanned leather, or leather with the smooth and supple hand of deerskin, deer-tanned cowhide, or kid works best for iron-on tranfers. Suede will not retain the transferred image.

Before you iron on the image, lay down a double thickness of mat board or a ½-inch thick (1.3 cm) foam board to create a hard, flat, heat-absorbing surface. Place a layer of newsprint paper between the iron and the transfer backing to prevent scorching.

Follow the manufacturer's instructions to apply heat with the iron. Your instructions should tell you whether or not to peel off the paper while the transfer is hot, or wait until the paper cools off.

Transfer Papers for Artists

A type of photo transfer paper is now on the market that can be used to transfer images to many surfaces, including leather. Different methods of transferring are used with different surfaces. (On leather, you can choose from a number of transferring methods outlined in the manufacturer's instructions, that include using acrylic medium or turpentine to transfer the image.)

Begin by copying the selected image onto the transfer paper with a black-and-white or color photocopier. Then cut away the excess paper from the image with a craft knife or scissors. The photo transfer is then placed in water for one minute. Once removed, carefully blot the tranfers between sheets of newsprint paper to remove the excess water. At this point, the image should slide easily off the paper (see project on pages 40 to 43 for more information.)

Decorative and Rubber Stamping

Before using stamps on leather or suede to make designs, you should always practice on a piece of the material that you'll be using for your project. By doing this, you'll test not only the quality of the stamped image, but the color and density of the ink that you choose.

Well-made stamps are a must for good results. Both rubber and decorative broad-based foam stamps work for stamping images on leather. (In general, rubber stamps will give you more detailed images, while broad-based foam stamps have larger patterns that work well for borders or repeating patterns.) To use your stamps over and over, take care to clean and store them properly.

Use a wedge-shaped cosmetic sponge or rubber printer's brayer to get a light, even application of dye or ink that will result in a sharp image (see page 15 for recommended inks). Apply firm pressure to the stamp when you apply it to the surface of the leather. Don't wiggle or rock the stamp, or the image might blur. The larger the stamp, the more pressure you'll need to apply across the entire stamp to make a clear, evenly delineated image. After

Rich, colorful patterns created with rubber stamps

stamping your image, lift the stamp straight up while holding down a corner of the leather or suede surface to keep the print from smearing. The prints made by stamps can also be accented with additional color made with markers (see page 15 for more information).

After stamping and coloring natural cowhide, deerskin, and rawhide, the surface must be sealed before the project is assembled. To do this, spray two light coats of spray acrylic leather finish on the surface to create a flexible, durable, water-repellent finish.

Stenciling

Precut stencils in a huge variety of styles, designs, and sizes are available on the market. The price of stencils varies according to their quality and detail. Some of the more expensive, detailed stencil designs are created by using a succession of several stencils that are registered to fit together. If you can't find a stencil that you like for your project, you can make up your own design that you transfer to thick drafting paper or stencil board before cutting it out with a craft knife.

After stenciling your design with stencil paints (see page 15 for more information), allow the paint to dry completely. If heat setting is recommended for your brand of paint, place brown paper or a pillowcase over the surface before pressing it with a heated iron.

Using a stencil brush to pounce paint between the lines of a stencil

Paint Finishes

Whether you opt to paint a simple colorful accent or an elaborate pattern on your leather or suede surface, the hand of the natural leather or suede surface doesn't have to be sacrificed. Certain paints, including stencil paints, will not change in appearance or crack with time if they are applied properly.

When painting on a sizeable area of leather or suede, you can use artist's acrylic paints with fabric medium or fabric paints with fabric medium. They are absorbed by the surface, and remain soft and flexible after drying.

A freehand design painted on leather

or silver metallic leaf. These thin sheets can be purchased in books and applied with special adhesive.

No matter what choice you make, you should always seal the surface of the leather with two coats of spray acrylic leather finish after applying metallic accents.

Photos on this page: Metallic accents applied to leather

Adding Metallic Accents

Easier and less expensive options than traditional gold and silver leafing now exist for adding metallic accents to leather. Smooth, sturdy, vegetable-tanned leather works best for this technique.

After completing any color work and finishing edge work, projects are ready for adding the gold or silver touch. The simplest way to apply a metallic accent, other than with metallic paint

and a brush, is to transfer a rub-on design (available in prepackaged sheets from craft supply stores).

Another option is a kit with water-based adhesive and a choice of gold or silver foil. The adhesive is applied with a brush, a cosmetic sponge (if using a stencil), or a rubber stamp.

If you want to make a project of heirloom quality, buy real or imitation gold

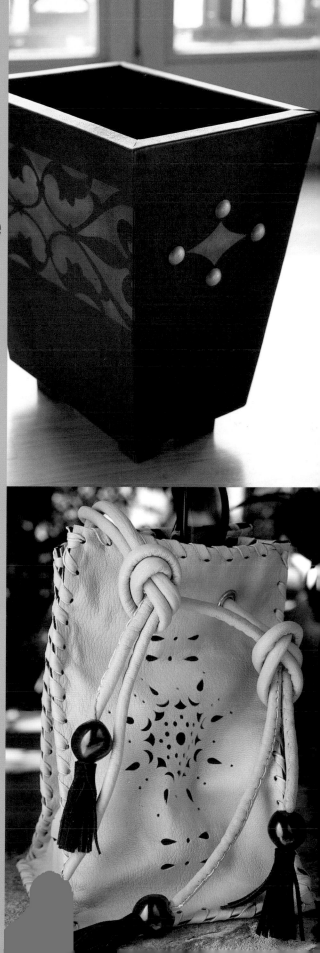

The following projects give you a breadth of choices that range from simple to complex. Leaf through the pages, study the projects you are attracted to, and choose one to begin with that fits your level of experience. Refer back to the front section of the book as needed.

CURTAIN TIEBACKS
WITH PAINTED DESIGNS

THIS SIMPLE-TO-MAKE TIEBACK CAN BE USED AS
AN ACCENT FOR ONE CURTAIN OR DUPLICATED FOR
A SERIES OF CURTAINS. USE OUR PAINTED
GEOMETRIC PATTERN OR DEVISE YOUR OWN TO FIT
YOUR PERSONAL DECOR. (THE PAINTED TABLE RUNNER
PICTURED MAKES A GREAT PARTNER FOR THESE TIEBACKS. SEE PAGES
36 AND 37 FOR THE DIRECTIONS.)

MATERIALS FOR ONE TIEBACK

Pattern (see page 130)

Piece of poster board

Tan-colored deer-tanned cowhide (2 square feet [.18 m²] per tieback)

Tan upholstery/nylon thread to match leather

5/16-inch (8 mm) brass grommets (2 per tieback)

Fabric paints: dark brown, black, white, metallic brown, metallic gold

Fabric paint medium

TOOLS AND SUPPLIES

Glue stick

Straightedge/ruler

Craft or "clicker" knife

Leather shears

Rubber cement

Sewing machine fitted with size 16 leather needle (or needle appropriate for your machine)

Punch board

1/4-inch (6 mm) round drive punch

Mallet

5/16-inch (8 mm) grommet setter

Old ceramic plate, sheet of glass, or other water-repellent surface to use as palette

Low-tack drafting tape

1/2-inch (1.3 cm) flat paintbrush

Fine-tip "liner" brush

INSTRUCTIONS

1. Use the glue stick to adhere the pattern to the poster board, and cut it out with the knife and straightedge.

2. Use the pattern and the knife to cut out as many sets of tiebacks as you wish from cowhide. Cut clip lines with leather shears as indicated on the pattern.

3. Place the tieback panels grain side down on the work surface. Baste a 1/2-inch (1.3 cm) hem along the long edges, easing the leather where the clip lines are cut. Glue and press the hem in place with rubber cement.

4. Use the sewing machine threaded with tan thread to topstitch a 1/4-inch (6 mm) seam along the basted edges (photo 1). Beginning at the end of each tieback, use leather shears to trim away the leather on both sides close to the stitching. (This process reduces the bulk of the leather later when you add the grommets.)

5. Fold over a hem of 1 inch (2.5 cm) on the two ends of each tieback, and baste in place with rubber cement. Place the tiebacks facedown on a punch board, and use a 1/4-inch (6 mm) round drive and mallet to punch holes in the center of the folded and basted ends.

6. Use the grommet setter to attach a grommet to both ends of each tieback (photo 2).

7. Squeeze small amounts of each fabric paint around the edge of your palette and some medium in the center. (Adding the medium allows more control with the paint while creating a translucent color on the surface.) Dip the flat paintbrush in water, and shake off the excess before dipping the brush in the medium.

8. Mask off dark brown squares as indicated on the pattern with drafting tape. Load the flat brush with dark brown paint, and paint in each square section. Allow the paint to dry, and remove the tape. Add highlights with the mixed metallic colors to the sides of each square.

9. Once the paint design dries, use the fine-tip "liner" brush loaded with black paint to paint a decorative triangular pattern over the squares. Add white highlight lines as shown in the finished piece (photo 3). Allow the paint to dry for 24 hours.

1

2

3

PAINTED TABLE RUNNER

CONTRASTING LEATHERS AND SHAPES ARE
SOFTENED BY DELICATE PAINTED FLOWERS ON THIS
BEAUTIFUL TABLE ACCENT. CARVED BONE BEADS
AND FRINGE ADD INTRIGUING VISUAL INTEREST.

MATERIALS

Patterns (see page 136)

Glue stick

Piece of poster board

3 square feet (.27 m²) of tan-colored
deer-tanned cowhide

4 square feet (.36 m²) of deer-tanned
black cowhide

Tan upholstery/nylon thread

20-inch-long (50.8 cm) piece of 2 mm
black round lace

4 carved bone beads (ours are
4½ inches [11.4 cm] long)

8-inch-long (20.3 cm) piece of 4-inch-
wide (10.2 cm) precut or handmade
black cowhide fringe

Fabric paints (we used dark brown,
reddish brown, black, ivory, metallic
brown, metallic white)

Fabric paint medium

TOOLS AND SUPPLIES

Craft or "clicker" knife

Straightedge/ruler

Rubber cement

Water-based white leather glue

Sewing machine fitted with size 16
leather needle (or needle appropriate
for your machine)

Palette for mixing paint (you can use
an old ceramic plate, sheet of glass,
or other nonabsorbent surface)

Fine-tip "liner" paintbrush

#5 round paintbrush

INSTRUCTIONS

1. Use the glue stick to adhere the patterns on the poster board. Use the knife to cut out durable patterns.

2. Use the knife and a straightedge to cut out the 8 x 40-inch (20.3 x 101.6 cm) main panel from the tan cowhide. Cut out two rounded side panels, two end tabs, and two ½ x 4-inch (1.3 x 10.2 cm) strips from the black cowhide.

3. Flip the main tan panel over onto your work surface so that the back is facing you. With the grain side down, overlap the black side panels on either long side of the panel, 1 inch (2.5 cm) from each edge in the center. Baste the overlapping seam in place with rubber cement, being careful not to get the cement on the front of the panel (photo 1).

4. Fold the two ½-inch-wide (1.3 cm) black strips in half, grain side out, and glue the doubled ends of each 1 inch (2.5 cm) inside the ends on the underside of the tan panel. Overlap and glue the rounded end tabs so that 1 inch (2.5 cm) is visible from the front (photo 2).

5. Thread the sewing machine with the tan thread. Flip the piece over so that it is grain side up. Stitch a ¼-inch (6 mm) seam all the way around the inside edge of the main panel, securing the side panels, folded strips, and end tabs.

6. Cut the black round lace in half, and thread each 10-inch (25.4 cm) length through the loops formed by the ½-inch-wide (1.3 cm) strips. Thread a bone bead onto each side of both lace lengths, and secure the beads with an overhand knot.

7. Cut the black fringe in half to form two 4-inch-long (10.2 cm) pieces. Place the pieces grain side down on your work sur-

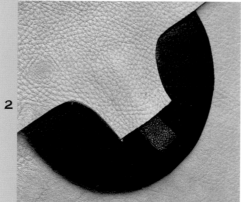

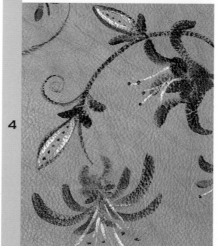

face. Spread a light coat of water-based white leather glue along the unfringed portion (bottom) of one of the pieces of black fringe. Tightly wrap the base of the fringe around the overhand knots and the ends of the round lace, overlapping tightly as you go. Repeat this process to add the other tassel to the opposite end of the runner (photo 3).

8. Pour out a bit of each of the paints onto your palette, and squeeze a bit of the fabric paint medium into the center. (During the process of painting in the next step, you'll dip each brush in water before mixing the medium with each color.)

9. Beginning in the center of the tan panel, use the fine-tip "liner" paintbrush to paint swirling lines that represent the stems of the flowers and the overall pattern, leaving about an 8-inch (20.3 cm)

margin on either side of the horizontal design. Add outlines of leaves to the stems with the fine-tip brush. Then use the round paintbrush to paint a loose flower design and add small, solid leaves. Use the fine-tip brush loaded with a light, contrasting color to add final highlights to the leaves and flowers (photo 4). Allow the finished paint design to dry about 24 hours before using.

Molded Leather Bowl

This simple form shows off the natural beauty of leather. Prop it up and display it as a decorative item, or fill it with festive red peppers or fruit to lend color to your table.

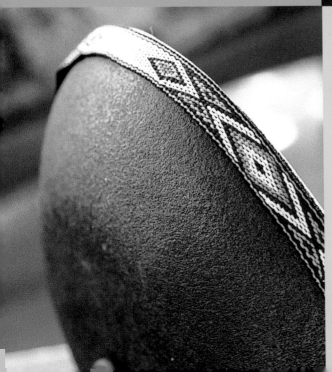

MATERIALS

Smooth, shallow bowl made of wood, thick glass, or plastic to use as mold (A variety of sizes will work. Do not use metal.)

2 square feet (.18 m²) of 8- to 9-ounce (3.18 to 3.58 mm) #1 grade double-shoulder cowhide

Tan-colored antique leather stain

Brown edge coat

Spray acrylic leather finish

Piece of decorative braided trim to fit outside edge of bowl (we used hitched webbing, an imitation horsehair braid)

TOOLS AND SUPPLIES

Scratch awl

Craft or "clicker" knife

Sponge

#2 edge beveler

Circle edge slicker

Rubber gloves

Wool scraps

Foam-tip brush

Cloth measuring tape

Leather shears

Contact cement

Leather-covered binder clips (see page 20)

Decorative iron plate holder (optional)

INSTRUCTIONS

1. Place the bowl facedown on the right side of the leather. Trace around the edge with the scratch awl.

2. Remove the bowl, and use the knife to cut out a leather disk, following the mark that you made.

3. Use a sponge and water to lightly dampen the edge around the disk. Use the #2 edge beveler to remove the corners from the disk's edge, and burnish it with the circle edge slicker. (If necessary, remoisten the edge before slicking it.)

4. Soak the leather in warm water until air bubbles no longer appear on the back side of the disk. Remove it from the water, and set it aside to dry partially. The leather is ready to form when the color of the leather is beginning to lighten to a pinkish color and the core of it is still damp. At this point, place the leather in the bowl (photo 1).

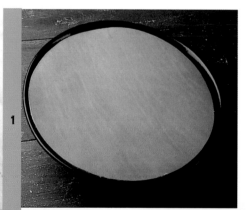

1

2

5. Use your fingers to repeatedly press, smooth, and form the leather into the bowl/mold (photo 2). Smooth out the edges. Once you've formed your leather bowl, lift it from the mold, and place it right side up on the work surface. Allow it dry completely.

6. Put on rubber gloves. Use a wool scrap to evenly apply the antique stain in a circular motion to the interior of the bowl. Allow it to dry completely. For a darker color, apply a second coat, and allow it to dry. Use the same process to apply antique stain to the exterior surface of the bowl.

7. Carefully apply brown edge coat along the top edge of the bowl with a foam-tip brush, and allow it to dry completely.

8. Apply two light coats of an acrylic leather finish to add a tough, water-repellent finish to the leather. Allow the finish to dry completely between coats.

9. To embellish the outside edge of your bowl, use the cloth measuring tape to determine the length of trim needed. Cut the trim to length using the leather shears. Apply a light, even coat of cement along the outside edge of the bowl that is no wider than the trim. Apply a coat of cement on the back side of the trim. Position and press the length of trim along the bowl's edge. Use the leather-covered clips to hold the trim in place until the cement sets. Place the bowl upright in the iron plate holder, or use it on flat on a surface to hold items of your choice (do not use it to hold anything wet).

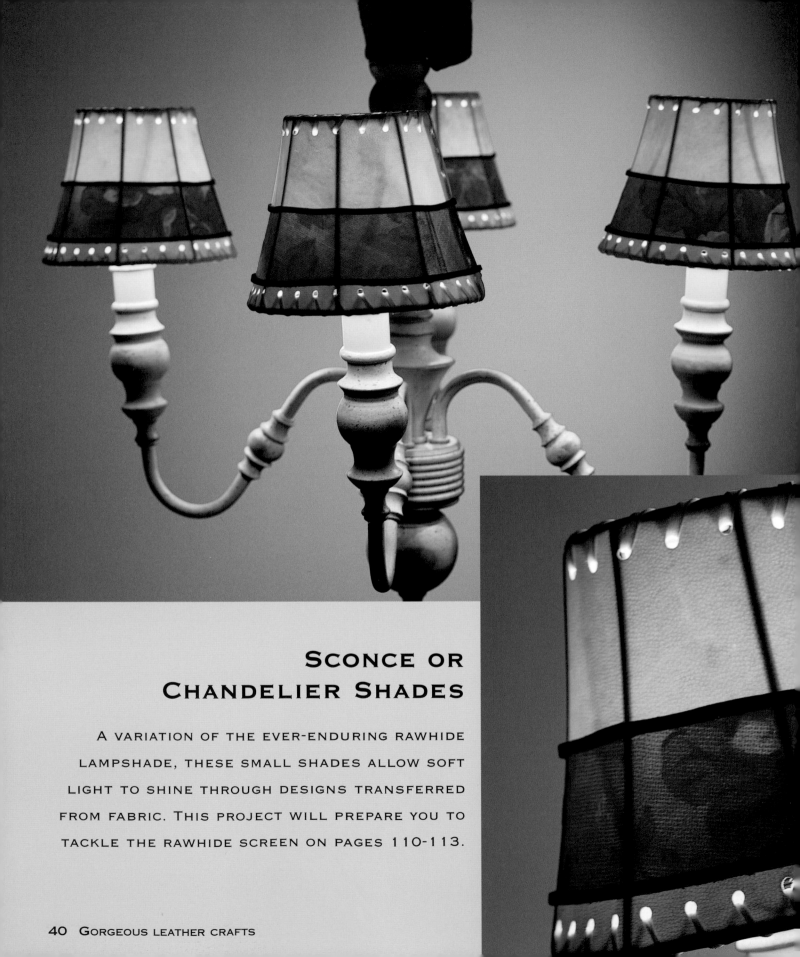

Sconce or Chandelier Shades

A variation of the ever-enduring rawhide lampshade, these small shades allow soft light to shine through designs transferred from fabric. This project will prepare you to tackle the rawhide screen on pages 110-113.

MATERIALS FOR EACH SHADE

Pattern for shade and trim (see page 131)

Piece of poster board

1 square foot (.09 m²) per shade of parchment rawhide

Wire lampshade frame (8-spoke frame shown has 3-inch-diameter [7.6 cm] top rim, 5-inch-diameter [12.7 cm] bottom rim, and is 4 inches [10.2 cm] tall)

1 yard (1.1 mm) rawhide lace

12 x 18-inch (30.5 x 45.7 cm) transfer paper made for artists (available at fine art supply stores)

16-inch (40.6 cm) long piece of printed fabric of your choice

Turpentine

1 yard (1.1 mm) brick red latigo lace

TOOLS AND SUPPLIES

Glue stick

Craft knife or "clicker" knife

Punch board

⅛-inch (3 mm) round drive punch

Mallet

Paper towels

Binder clips

Clothespins

Leather shears

2-prong lacing needle

Small foam paint roller

Newsprint paper

Contact cement

Toothpick

(see page 131)

INSTRUCTIONS

1. Use the glue stick to glue the pattern onto a piece of poster board, and cut it out with the knife.

2. Place the punch board on your work surface, and use the drive punch and mallet to punch out the holes as marked on the pattern.

3. Prepare the rawhide by soaking it in water until it is pliable. Remove it from the water, and pat it dry with paper towels.

4. Use the poster board pattern and knife to cut out the shade cover from the rawhide. Use binder clips to secure the pattern to the rawhide before punching out the holes along the edges as indicated (photo 1).

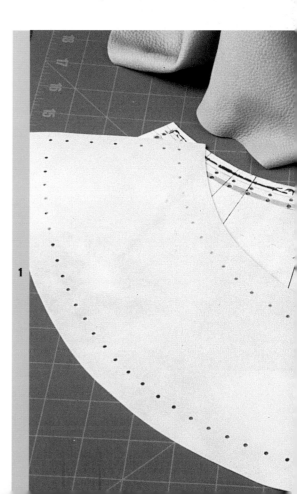

1

5. Position the rawhide on the wire frame with the holes positioned about ¼ inch (6 mm) from the top and the bottom of the frame, allowing about ⅛-inch (3 mm) of rawhide to overlap the top and bottom of the frame. Hold the rawhide in place with clothespins (photo 2). (Where the two ends of the shade meet, they should overlap about ½ inch [1.3 cm]).

6. Use the leather shears to cut off a 10-inch (25.4 cm) piece of rawhide lace. Soak the lace in water until it is pliable. Open the two-prong lacing needle with a knife and insert the end of the lace (photo 3).

7. At the top of the shade, thread the rawhide lace through the first hole where the leather overlaps, loop the lace over the top of the shade, and pull it back through the adjacent hole to the front of the shade. Leave a short tail to tie off later, and hold it in place with a clothespin (photo 4).

8. Whipstitch the rawhide lace around the top edge, pulling the lace snug but not tight (photo 5). When you reach the starting point make an overhand knot in the lace ends to secure them inside the shade. (As the rawhide dries, it will shrink around the wire frame until it is stiff and taut. If you pull the stitches too tight, the wire frame will bow.)

9. Use the same technique to secure the bottom edge of the rawhide to the frame with a 15-inch (38.1 cm) piece of lace, using an overhand knot to secure the lace ends.

2
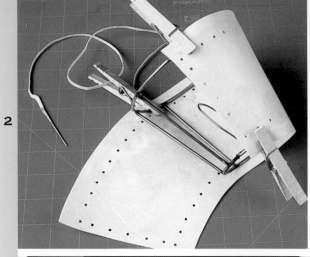

3

4
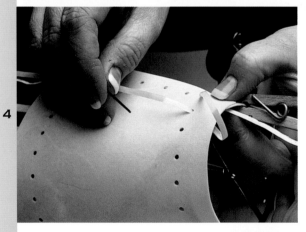

5
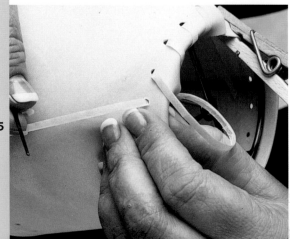

TIP: Do not use a bulb with wattage higher than 60 with this shade.

10. Cut a 10-inch (25.4 cm) length of rawhide lace for the vertical side seam. Soak the rawhide lace until pliable, and attach the two-prong lacing needle.

11. Use a double running stitch to secure the side seam by threading the rawhide lace through the first hole at the top of the shade to the hole at the bottom edge and back up the side seam. Secure the ends with an overhand knot.

12. Allow the rawhide shade to dry completely (approximately 48 hours).

13. Following the manufacturer's instructions on the transfer paper, use a photocopy machine to copy the selected fabric image onto the paper.

14. Cut out the transfer band from the shade pattern, and use it to cut out the trim from the transfer paper. Soak the transfer image in water for one minute.

15. Use the foam roller to apply a even coat of turpentine to the surface of the shade (photo 6).

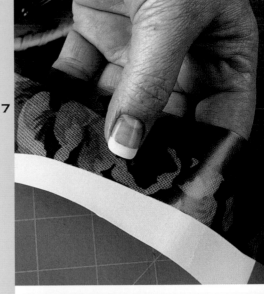

7

16. Lift the transfer from the water, and place it between two sheets of newsprint paper to remove the excess water. Carefully slide the transfer film off the paper backing (photo 7).

17. With the rawhide shade on its side, carefully begin to press the transfer film onto the rawhide shade about ⅛ inch (3 mm) above the bottom laced area where the overlapping seam is. Place your hand inside the shade and slowly rotate it as you position the film on the surface (photo 8).
Warning: The film will quickly adhere to the rawhide surface, so repositioning the image is not an option.

18. Use the roller to carefully reapply a thin, even coat of turpentine over the transfer film. Allow it to dry.

19. Cut two strips of latigo lace to fit around the top and bottom edge of the shade's transfer design. Use the toothpick to apply contact cement to the back side of each lace length, and press it into place on the shade (photo 9). Allow it to dry.

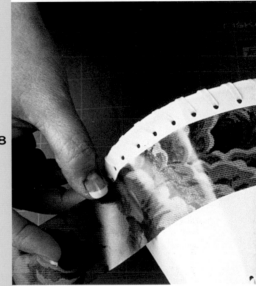

8

9

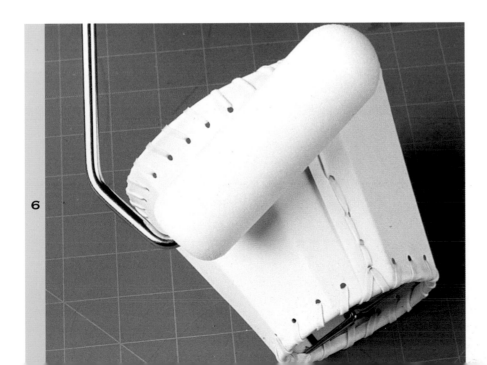

6

MOLDED CHARGER PLATES

A VARIATION ON THE LEATHER BOWL DESCRIBED ON PAGES 38 AND 39, THESE CHARGER PLATES SERVE AS A TASTEFUL BACKGROUND FOR YOUR DINNERWARE AND FOOD.

MATERIALS FOR FOUR CHARGER PLATES

Wood, plastic, or glass (no metal) charger plate, larger than the dinner plates you intend to use

6 square feet (.54 m²) of 8- to 9-ounce (3.18 to 3.58 mm) #1 grade double-shoulder leather

Leather solvent-based "spirit" dye in black

Spray acrylic leather finish

TOOLS AND SUPPLIES

Wing divider

Craft or "clicker" knife

Sponge

#2 edge beveler

Circle edge slicker

Rubber gloves

Wool scraps

Rag (old T-shirt or soft cotton cloth)

INSTRUCTIONS

1. Place the charger plate facedown on the right side of the leather. Carefully move the divider around the plate, allowing the outside arm of the wing divider to scratch a guideline in the leather that is ½ inch (1.3 m) larger than the circumference of the charger.

2. Use the knife to cut out a leather disk, following the guideline that you drew (photo 1).

3. Use a sponge and water to lightly dampen the edge around the leather disk. Use the edge beveler to remove the corners. Burnish the edges with the circle edge slicker, remoistening the edge as needed.

4. Soak the leather in warm water until the air bubbles no longer appear on the back side of the leather. Remove the leather from the water, and set it aside to dry partially. The leather is ready to form when the color of the leather is beginning to lighten to a pinkish color and the core of the leather is still damp.

5. Use your fingers repeatedly to press, smooth, and form the leather into the charger plate (photo 2). Once the leather charger has been formed, lift it from the mold, and place it upside down on the work surface. Allow it to dry completely.

6. Put on rubber gloves. Use the wool to evenly and thoroughly apply the black spirit dye in a circular motion on the front of the leather charger. Allow the dye to dry completely.

7. Place the leather charger on the front of the charger plate again. With an old T-shirt or soft cotton cloth, use a side-to-side and circular motion to buff the entire top surface of the leather charger. This will remove the excess pigment.

8. Apply a second application of dye to achieve a richer color, and allow the leather to dry completely. Buff the surface again.

9. Repeat steps 6 through 8 to dye the back of the leather charger, placing it on the back side of the charger plate for support.

10. Spray on two light coats of acrylic finish to both sides of the leather charger to add a tough, water-repellent finish. Allow the finish to dry completely between coats.

11. Follow the same steps to create three more leather chargers.

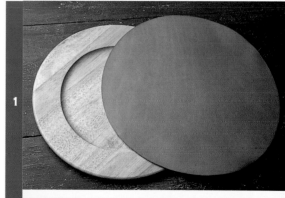

Branded and Painted Place Mats

These cheerful mats embellished with burned and painted designs illustrate a contemporary use of the traditional technique of branding. Silver and glass beads strung on leather lace add glimmering accents. (The accompanying napkin cuffs pictured are described on page 50.)

MATERIALS FOR FOUR PLACE MATS

Piece of poster board

Place mat design and hole-punch patterns (see page 131)

12 square feet (1.1 m²) of 6- to 7-ounce (2.39 to 2.78 mm) vegetable-tanned leather

50 decorative silver beads (for each place mat)

100 seed beads in two contrasting colors (for each place mat)

Fabric paints: yellow, orange, green, purple, and red

Fabric paint medium

Old ceramic plate, piece of glass, or paper plate to use as palette

Leather wax

22½ yards (20 m) 1 mm round leather lace, natural-colored

TOOLS AND SUPPLIES

Craft or "clicker" knife

Straightedge/ruler

Punch board

Mallet

¹⁄₁₆ - and ⁵⁄₃₂-inch (1.6 and 4 mm) round hole drive punches

Fine-tip black marker

Tracing film

Sponge

Stylus tool

Clay modeling tool with spoon tip (optional)

Woodburning tool with bullet-shaped, angled, and circular tip

Fine-grit sandpaper

Needle-nose pliers

Small and medium-sized paintbrushes

Hair blow dryer

Soft cloth

Horsehair shoe brush

Leather shears

1. Use the craft knife and straightedge to cut out a 14 x 20-inch (35.6 x 50.8 cm) piece of poster board. Refer to the punch-hole pattern provided to mark the position of the holes on the poster board with the marker. Use the punch board, mallet, and $^1/_{16}$-inch (1.6 mm) drive punch to punch out the holes.

2. Use the marker to trace the design pattern onto the tracing film.

3. Place the leather grain side up on the work surface. Using the poster board pattern as a guide, cut out four rectangular place mats with your knife and straightedge.

4. Dampen the sponge with water, and lightly moisten the front of one of the cut pieces of leather. Place the tracing film with design on top of it. Press along the lines of the design with the stylus tool to transfer them. Repeat this process on the other three pieces. Allow all of the leather pieces to dry completely. (If you accidentally mark a line on the leather surface that you do not want, rub out the line with your finger or the spoon end of the modeling tool.)

5. Insert the large bullet-shaped tip into the woodburner, and heat it up. Brand the rectangular border lines (photo 1) and the dots in the center of the mats with this tip. Remove the tip with the pliers, and insert the angled tip (photo 2). Use the angled tip to burn the decorative petal shapes (photo 3), the multiple line patterns in

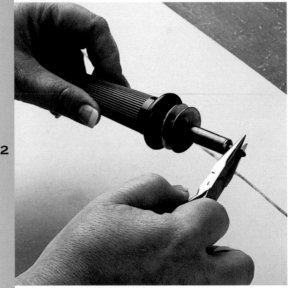

the center section of the mat, and the harsh marks along the left and right sides of the mats. Rub the woodburning tips between sandpaper to clean them as needed. Change the tip to a circular one, and use that tip to brand the shapes within the petals.

6. Referring to the pattern, use the 1/16-inch (1.6 mm) drive punch and the mallet to punch the holes needed for adding beads along the left and right sides of each place mat. Use the 5/32-inch (4 mm) drive punch and the mallet to punch the random pattern of holes within the center rectangle of each place mat.

7. Squeeze out dollops of paints onto your palette with a bit of fabric paint medium in the center. Mix a small amount of medium with each paint color before enhancing the branded designs on the placemats (photo 4). (See finished photos for suggestions of color use.) Allow the paint to dry for 24 hours.

8. Apply a coat of leather wax to the face of the place mats, and buff it with a soft cloth to achieve a mellow finish. (If any white lines appear after buffing, apply low heat to the area with a blow-

TIP: To achieve alternating lengths of fringe, vary the position of the knots slightly on each lace length. To relax the lace, wet the lengths slightly with water, and pull the lace down.

dryer to loosen the wax. With a horse-hair shoe brush, buff the leather surface to remove the wax buildup.)

9. Use the leather shears to cut fifty 4-inch (10.2 cm) lengths of 1 mm round lace for each place mat. Make an overhand knot on one end of each

lace length, and thread one decorative silver bead and two contrasting colored seed beads onto each length.

10. Thread a lace end through each of the holes on the top of the place mat, and tie off on the back with another overhand knot (photo 5). Repeat steps 9 and 10 for each place mat.

Branded and Painted Napkin Cuffs

Curvilinear shapes echoing the designs of the accompanying placemats (see pages 46-49) inspired these functional napkin holders.

MATERIALS

Pattern (see page 132)

Sheet of poster board

1 square foot (.09 m²) of 6- to 7-ounce (2.39 to 2.78 mm) vegetable-tanned leather

Fabric paints: yellow, orange, green, purple, and red

Fabric paint medium

Paper plate or other palette

Leather wax

16-inch-long (40.6 cm) piece of 1 mm round leather lace, natural-colored

Beads of your choice that fit onto 1 mm lace (we used one decorative silver bead and two colored seed beads for each cuff to match the beads used on the placemats)

TOOLS AND SUPPLIES

Glue stick

Craft or "clicker" knife

Punch board

½-inch (1.3 cm) oblong drive punch

Mallet

Black fine-tip marker

Tracing film

Sponge

Stylus tool

Clay modeling tool with spoon-shaped end or wooden craft stick (optional)

Woodburning tool with bullet-shaped tip

Small and medium-sized paintbrushes

Old ceramic plate, sheet of glass, or paper plate to use as palette

Soft cloth

Wool scraps

Hair blow dryer (optional)

Horsehair shoe brush (optional)

Fine-grit sandpaper

1/16-inch (1.6 mm) round hole drive punch

Leather shears

INSTRUCTIONS

1. Glue the pattern to a sheet of poster board, and cut it out with the knife. Place the punch board on your work surface. Mark and punch the position of the ½-inch (1.3 cm) oblong slit with the oblong punch and mallet.

2. Place the leather grain side up on your work surface. Position the poster board on the leather surface, and cut around it with the knife. Repeat to cut out three more pieces. (Making several cuts will result in jagged edges. For a smooth edge, cut completely through the leather with one continuous movement.)

3. Use the fine-tip marker to trace the design pattern onto the tracing film.

4. Dampen the sponge with water, and lightly moisten the fronts of the cut pieces of leather (cuffs). Use a stylus tool to trace the decorative pattern onto the cuffs from the tracing film. Allow the leather to dry completely. (If you accidentally mark a line on the leather that you don't want, you can rub away the line with the spoon-shaped end of the clay modeling tool.)

5. Insert a bullet-shaped tip into the woodburning tool. Brand the leather with the tool by tracing the transferred lines to create the decorative pattern. Use sandpaper to clean the tool as needed during the process of burning the leather (photo 1).

6. Apply fabric paints and fabric medium to your palette. Mix a bit of fabric medium with each color before painting loose designs on the cuffs. Allow it to dry.

7. Apply leather wax to the surface with wool scraps to lend a mellow finish. Allow it to dry, then buff or polish the surfaces with a soft cloth. (If any white lines appear after buffing, apply low heat to the area with a blow-dryer to loosen the wax. With a horsehair shoe brush, buff the leather surface to remove the wax buildup.)

8. Use the clay modeling tool or wooden craft stick to smooth the edges around each napkin cuff. (If the edges are really rough around the curves, use the sandpaper to lightly smooth them out first.)

9. On top of the punch board, use the 1/16-inch (1.6 mm) drive punch and mallet to punch a hole in the tip of each of the cuff's swirls.

10. To create the loop to hold the napkin, fold the tip of the leather cuff through each oblong slit (photo 2).

11. Cut the 1 mm round lace into four equal pieces with the leather shears, and tie one end with an overhand knot. Thread them through the back of the holes at the end of each cuff. Slide beads onto each piece of lace, and tie off with an overhand knot to hold them in place.

GOLD-EMBELLISHED DESK SET

UPGRADE YOUR DESK FROM PLAIN TO SOPHISTICATED WITH THREE HANDSOME PIECES.

MATERIALS

1 square foot (.09 m²) of 9- to 10-ounce (3.58 to 3.9 mm) #1 or #2 vegetable-tanned leather

Antique leather stain in tan

Brown edge coat

Precut stencil with initial of your choice

Imitation gold leaf kit with adhesive (available at craft supply stores)

Spray acrylic leather finish

TOOLS AND SUPPLIES

Craft or "clicker knife"

Straightedge/ruler

Paper or plastic to protect work surface

Rubber gloves

Wool scraps

Sponge

#2 edge beveler

Circle edge slicker

1-inch (2.5 cm) foam-tip brush

Sticky notes or low-tack drafting tape

Wedge-shaped cosmetic sponge

GOLD-FOILED MOUSE PAD

PERSONALIZE YOUR MOUSE PAD WITH A GOLD-LEAFED INITIAL OF YOUR CHOICE.

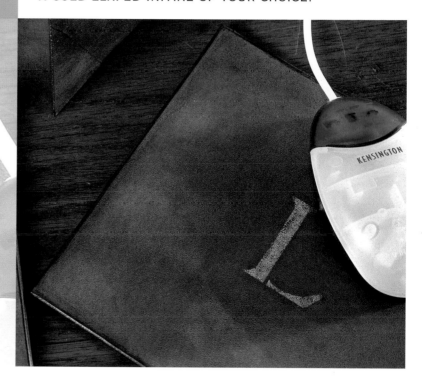

INSTRUCTIONS

1. Use a straightedge and a knife to cut out a 7½ x 8½-inch (19.1 x 21.6 cm) piece from the leather.

2. Cover the work space with sheets of paper or plastic. Wearing a pair of rubber gloves, use wool scraps to apply an even coat of antique stain to the surface of the leather (photo 1).

3. Use the sponge to lightly moisten one edge with water (photo 2). Use a #2 edge beveler to round both sides of the edges (photo 3), and smooth the edge with the circle edge slicker (photo 4). Repeat this step for the three remaining edges.

4. Use a foam-tip brush to apply brown edge coat to all four edges (photo 5).

5. Position the stencil in the center of the mouse pad, and hold it in place with the sticky notes or low-tack tape. Use a cosmetic sponge to dab the adhesive for the gold foil in the open areas of the stencil. After a couple of minutes, apply a second coat of adhesive.

6. Remove the stencil, and press the foil facedown onto the tacky adhesive (photo 6). Remove the foil backing, and spray two coats of leather finish over the surface (photo 7).

TIP: As an alternative to the foil, use imitation or real gold leaf sheets. After pressing the leaf onto the surface, use a soft brush to lightly dust away the excess leaf.

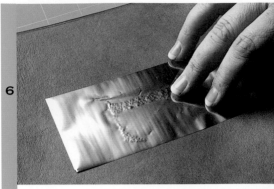

NOTEPAPER HOLDER

TRANSFORM A WOODEN BOX INTO A THING OF BEAUTY FOR STORING PAPERS AND OTHER DESK ITEMS.

MATERIALS

2½ square feet (.22 m²) of 3- to 4-ounce (84 to 112 g) vegetable-tanned leather

Unfinished wooden notepaper holder (available at craft and home decorating stores)

Piece of poster board

Antique leather stain in tan

Brown edge coat

Water-based wood sealer

Brown acrylic paint

Water-based satin varnish

Rub-on design sheet in gold (available at craft and art supply stores)

Spray acrylic leather finish

TOOLS AND SUPPLIES

Pencil

Craft knife or "clicker" knife

Paper or plastic to protect work surface

Rubber gloves

Wool scraps

Straightedge/ruler

Sponge

#1 edge beveler

Circle edge slicker

1-inch (2.5 cm) foam-tip brush

1-inch (2.5 cm) flat paintbrush

Fine-grit sandpaper

Contact cement

Clay modeling tool with spoon-shaped end

INSTRUCTIONS

1. Position one of the sides of the notepaper holder on the poster board. Trace around the edge with a pencil. (If your holder is not perfectly square, trace an additional pattern to represent the other two sides.) Cut out the durable pattern(s) with the knife.

2. Cover your work surface with paper or plastic. Wearing rubber gloves, use wool scraps to rub an even coat of antique leather stain over an area of the leather large enough to cut out the four panels needed to cover the holder. Allow the leather to dry completely.

3. Use the pattern(s), straightedge, and knife to cut out the four leather panels.

4. Position the panels against the sides of the box to make sure they fit. Select an edge of each panel to be the top edge. Use the sponge and water to lightly moisten each top edge. Bevel the outside edge of each piece with the #1 edge beveler, and smooth with the circle edge slicker.

5. Use the foam-tip brush to apply brown edge coat to all the edges of the panels.

6. Use the flat brush to apply water-based wood sealer to the interior, top edge, the corners of the four sides, and the bottom of the holder. Wash the brush out with water, and allow the holder to dry. Sand the areas that you sealed, and remove the dust.

7. Use the flat brush to apply two coats of brown acrylic paint over the sealed and sanded areas, and allow the paint to dry between coats. Apply a coat of water-based varnish to all of the same areas except the corners of the four sides (photo 1).

8. Apply an even coat of contact cement to the backs of each of the four panels and each matching side of the holder. Position and press each leather panel into place on the holder (photo 2). Allow the holder to dry overnight.

9. Use the knife to cut out the transfer designs for each leather panel. Carefully position one of the designs on a panel. Use the smooth side of the modeling tool to transfer the design from its sheet (photo 3). Carefully peel away the sheet (photo 4). Repeat to add designs to each side of the holder.

10. Apply two coats of spray acrylic leather finish to the outside of the holder.

MATERIALS

4 square feet (.36 m²) of 9- to 10-ounce (3.58 to 3.9 mm) #1 or #2 grade cowhide carving shoulder

Antique leather stain in tan

Brown edge coat

Rub-on design sheet in gold with design of your choice (available at craft and art supply stores)

Spray acrylic leather finish

TOOLS AND SUPPLIES

Paper or plastic to protect work surface

Pencil

Straightedge/ruler

Rubber gloves

Wool scraps

Craft or "clicker" knife

Sponge

#2 edge beveler

Circle edge slicker

1-inch (2.5 cm) foam-tip brush

Fine-tip black marker

V-gouge

Skiver

#4 French edger tool

Modeling tool with spoon-shaped end

Contact cement

Stack of books

DESK PAD

THIS HANDSOME DESK PAD IS HIGHLIGHTED BY LEATHER PANELS WITH RUB-ON GOLD DESIGNS.

INSTRUCTIONS

1. Cover your work surface with paper or plastic. Place the leather on top of the protected surface. Wearing rubber gloves, use wool scraps to rub an even coat of antique leather stain over an area of the leather large enough to cut out a 15 x 22-inch (38.1 x 55.9 cm) panel and two 3 x 18-inch (7.6 x 45.7 cm) leather panels. Allow the leather to dry completely.

2. Use a knife and straightedge to cut out the leather panels.

3. Use a sponge to lightly moisten an edge of the large panel. Use the #2 edge beveler to bevel both sides of the edge. Smooth the edge with a circle edge slicker. Repeat this process for the other three sides of the large panel and the long sides of the two narrow panels (leaving the short ends unfinished).

4. Use the foam-tip brush to paint all the beveled edges with brown edge coat.

5. Place the long panels facedown on the work surface. Measure 1½ inches (3.8 cm) from each end of both, and mark a guideline with the fine-tip black marker. Set the blade of the V-gouge to cut halfway through the leather. With the straightedge as a guide, cut along the lines to mark off the folds on the end of each long panel (photo 1).

6. Use the French edger tool (photo 2) and the skiver (photo 3) to thin the leather from the fold to the end of each panel (about 1 inch [2.5 cm] of leather) as well as the unfinished edges. Moisten the leather as needed. (The resulting leather ends should be about the thickness of heavy paper.)

7. Wet the beveled ends, and fold them over (photo 4). Press them firmly, and allow them to dry completely in a folded position (photo 5).

8. Cut out the transfer designs to fit the length of each of the side panels. Carefully position the designs gold side down on the front of each panel. (Keep in mind that once you place the transfer onto the leather it is very hard to remove.) Use the smooth side of a spooned modeling tool to rub the design onto the leather. Carefully peel off each backing sheet.

9. Spray two coats of the spray acrylic leather finish on the decorated panels.

10. Slide the molded leather panels on either end of the desk pad (photo 6). Place the assembled pad upside down on the work surface. Secure the folded-over ends of the side panels with contact cement. Weight the edges with a stack of books, and allow them to dry overnight.

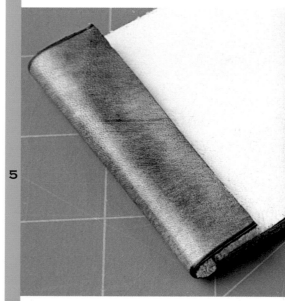

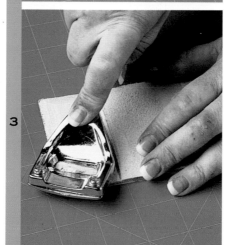

No-Sew Woven Pillows

A SIMPLE WEAVING TECHNIQUE
TRANSFORMS LUSCIOUS STRIPS
OF SUEDE INTO HANDSOME
PILLOW COVERS STUDDED WITH
BLACK RIVETS.

MATERIALS

7 square feet (.63 m²) of tobacco-colored garment cowhide suede

3 square feet (.27 m²) of chocolate-colored garment cowhide suede

1.5 square feet (.14 m²) of black garment cowhide suede

Large sheet of mat board (available at office supply or craft stores)

Steel double-cap black rivets with ¼-inch (6 mm) cap, post, and base

12-inch (30.5 cm) square pillow form

12 x 16-inch (30.5 x 40.6 cm) rectangular pillow form

TOOLS AND SUPPLIES

Craft or "clicker" knife

Fine-tip black marker

Binder clips (available at office supply stores)

Syringe applicator with tapered tip (available in art and craft supply stores)

Water-based white leather adhesive

Books or object to use as a weight

Straightedge/ruler

Rivet setter

Concave anvil strip

Contact cement

³⁄₃₂-inch (2.4 mm) round hole drive punch

Mallet

Punch board

INSTRUCTIONS

1. Place the suede on your work surface. Use the knife to cut the strips for the pillow fronts, as described below:

For 12 x 12-inch (30.5 x 30.5 cm) pillow:

1½ x 13-inch (3.8 x 33 cm) strips of suede (2 of tobacco, 2 of chocolate)

1 x 13-inch (2.5 x 33 cm) strips of suede (4 of black, 6 of chocolate, 10 of tobacco)

For 12 x 16-inch (30.5 x 40.6 cm) pillow:

1½ x 17-inch (3.8 x 43.2 cm) strips of suede (2 of tobacco, 2 of chocolate)

1 x 13-inch (2.5 x 33 cm) strips of suede (14 of tobacco)

1 x 17-inch (2.5 x 43.2 cm) strips of suede (4 of black and 6 of chocolate)

2. From the tobacco-colored suede, cut one pillow backing that measures 13 x 13 inches (33 x 33 cm) and one that measures 13 x 17 inches (33 x 43.2 cm).

3. Use the knife to cut two pieces of mat board: one that measures 14 x 14 inches (35.6 x 35.6 cm) and another that measures 14 x 18 inches (35.6 x 45.7 cm). Inside each board, draw a line with the marker that is ½ inch (1.3 cm) from the edge all the way around to serve as a guideline.

4. To begin the square pillow, place one of the 1½ x 13-inch (3.8 x 33 cm) tobacco-colored strips faceup (grain or right side up) along one edge of the square piece of mat board, inside the guideline that you marked. Then place the 1 x 13-inch (2.5 x 33 cm) strips of tobacco-colored suede right side up next to one another beside this first strip. Place the remaining 1½ x 13-inch (3.8 x 33 cm) strip grain side up at the end.

5. For the rectangular pillow, repeat this process, placing the 1½ x 17-inch (3.8 x 43.2 cm) tobacco-colored strips right side up inside each outside edge of the guideline, and the 1 x 17-inch (2.5 x 43.2 cm) tobacco-colored strips inside.

6. Arrange the chocolate and black strips grain side up on the work surface by color in the order to be weaved on the front pillow cover.

7. On each of the pillows, weave one of the 1½-inch-wide (3.8 cm) chocolate-colored strips over and under along one end of the tobacco strips. Secure the ends of the strips with binder clips.

8. Weave the remaining chocolate and black strips, using the clips to secure the starting end of each strip while weaving (photo 1). (To create the pattern shown in the photo, weave one black strip next to the 1½-inch-wide [3.8 cm] chocolate-colored strip followed by two chocolate strips.)

9. Pull the slack from all strips, and use binder clips to clamp them securely in place (photo 2). (Because the suede will stretch slightly, don't worry if some of the strips' ends extend beyond the drawn guidelines.)

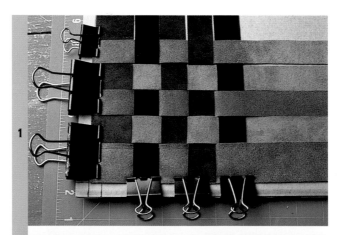

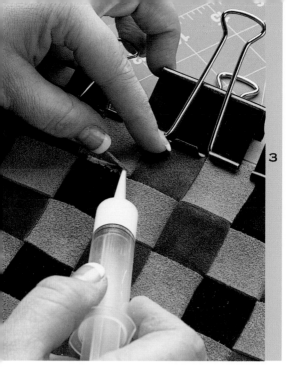

3

14. Place the punch board on your work surface. Use a 3/32-inch (2.4 mm) drive punch and mallet to punch one hole in each corner that is 3/8 inch (9.5 mm) from the edge, followed by two holes on each side of the corner hole the same distance from the edge. Around the edges of the covers, leave a 3/8-inch (9.5 mm) margin, punching

two holes within the boundaries of each remaining strip (photo 4).

15. Set the double-cap rivets along the three basted edges using a rivet setter and a concave anvil (photo 5).

16. Place each pillow form into the appropriate pillow cover. Set rivets along the open edges to secure the forms.

10. Use a tapered-tip syringe to inject a small, even amount of white leather adhesive between the layers of strips (photo 3). Place a weight (such as a couple of books) over the woven suede surfaces until they are completely dry.

11. Remove the binder clips. Use the knife and straightedge to trim the uneven edges of the woven pillow fronts as needed.

12. If you want to decorate the surface of one or both of your woven pillow fronts with rivets, use the rivet setter and concave anvil to punch holes and set the double-cap rivets in a pattern.

13. Place the pillow fronts and backings together with the right sides out. Cement three of the sides of each together, 1/2 inch (1.3 cm) from the edge.

4

5

MATERIALS

Unfinished wooden tray (this style available at craft supply stores)

Water-based wood sealer

Acrylic paints (dark green, black, metallic gold, and bronze)

Satin varnish

Piece of poster board

2- to 3-ounce (.78 to 1.19 mm) vegetable-tanned leather (trim pieces)

Antique leather stain in medium brown

Rubber stamps of your choice

Spray acrylic leather finish

3/32-inch (2.4 mm) black leather lace

Contact cement or water-based white leather adhesive

STAMPED VALET

A PAINTED WOODEN TRAY IS ENHANCED WITH A WHIPSTITCHED LINING MADE OF STAINED AND STAMPED LEATHER. GREAT FOR HOLDING THE PERSONAL EFFECTS OF BOTH GUYS AND GALS.

INSTRUCTIONS

1. Sand the wooden tray to remove any rough spots, and wipe it off with the tack cloth. Apply a coat of the wood sealer with the flat paintbrush, and allow it to dry. Sand it again lightly, and clean it with the tack cloth.

2. Use the flat paintbrush to apply two coats of dark green acrylic paint to the tray, allowing it to dry between coats. Apply one to two coats of satin varnish on top of the painted wood.

3. Use the craft knife and straightedge to cut a piece of poster board to fit the bottom of the tray. Mark with a guideline ⅛ inch (3 mm) inside the edge. Make marks that are ¼ inch (6 mm) apart all the way around the guideline. Use the ³⁄₃₂-inch (2.4 mm) lacing chisel to make a series of slits where the marks are that will indicate where to whipstitch the leather.

4. Use the knife to cut out a piece of leather that is ½ inch (1.3 cm) wider and longer than the tray's bottom. (The leather will shrink after you stain it.)

5. Put on the rubber gloves, and use the wool scrap to apply antique leather stain to the front surface of the leather piece with a circular motion. Allow the stain to dry, and then apply a second coat.

6. Use a wedge-shaped cosmetic sponge to apply a thin coat of black paint to each rubber stamp before stamping detailed impressions on the surface in a random design.

7. Use the fine-tip "liner" paintbrush to add metallic gold and bronze painted accents to the stamped impressions (photo 1).

8. Use the poster board pattern and knife to trim the stained leather piece to fit inside the tray. Then use the single-prong lacing chisel and mallet to punch the ³⁄₃₂-inch (2.4 mm) slits required for lacing. Use the foam-tip brush to apply stain along the edges to give them a finished look.

9. Seal the leather with two coats of spray acrylic leather finish.

10. Thread the two-prong lacing needle with a length of black leather lace that is three times the distance around the edge of the tray. Pull the thread from the back to the front at one of the corner holes, leaving a 1-inch (2.5 cm) tail. Whipstitch a couple of stitches, and then secure the tail under those stitches. Whipstitch all the way around the edge. To complete the lacing, thread the lace underneath the last two stitches, and snip off the excess lace with the leather shears.

11. Apply a thin, even coat of cement or adhesive to the backside of the leather, and press it down inside the tray (photo 2). Place a weight on top of the leather while it dries.

TOOLS AND SUPPLIES

Fine-grit sandpaper

Tack cloth

1-inch (2.5 cm) flat paintbrush

Craft knife or "clicker" knife

Straightedge/ruler

Pencil

³⁄₃₂-inch (2.4 mm) single-prong lacing chisel

Rubber gloves

Wool scraps

Wedge-shaped cosmetic sponges

Fine-tip "liner" paintbrush

Mallet

1-inch (2.5 cm) foam-tip brush

Punch board

Two-prong lacing needle

Leather shears

TOOLED FRAME

THE LEATHER ON THIS BEAUTIFUL FRAME IS TOOLED
WITH A VARIETY OF TRADITIONAL STAMPING TOOLS
TO CREATE A RICHLY PATTERNED SURFACE.

MATERIALS

Patterns for cutting front and back as well as stitching holes, if using the same frame that we did (see page 132)

Sheet of poster board

2 square feet (.18m²) of 3- to 4-ounce (1.19 to 1.6mm) vegetable-tanned leather

Wooden arched frame with 4 x 6-inch (10.2 x 15.2 cm) window (this is a standard shape available at craft stores)

Red acrylic paint

Leather wax

Natural, full-grain leather lace

Brown waxed thread

TOOLS AND SUPPLIES

Glue stick

Craft or "clicker" knife

Pencil

Scratch awl

1/16-inch (1.6 mm), 5/16-inch (8mm), and 1/4-inch (6 mm) round hole drive punches

Mallet

Punch board

Cloth measuring tape

Straightedge/ruler

Sponge

Tracing film

Stylus tool

Swivel knife

Stamping tools: two styles and sizes of veiner tools, camouflage tool, seed tool, beveler tool

Fine-tip "liner" paintbrush

Hair blow dryer (optional)

Horsehair shoe brush

Two-prong lacing needle

Contact cement

4 x 6-inch (10.2 x 15.2 cm) piece of glass or plastic sheet

Photo or other image trimmed to 4 x 6 inches (10.2 x 15.2 cm)

4 x 6-inch (10.2 x 15.2 cm) piece of foamboard

Sponge

Soft cloth

INSTRUCTIONS

1. Use the glue stick to adhere the patterns to the poster board. Use the knife to cut out the two shapes, including the window on the front. Use the pencil to mark the position of the hole near the bottom of the frame back. (The hole is made in this particular frame for inserting a dowel on which to prop the frame if you want to place it upright on a surface.)

2. Use the awl to pierce small holes on the front of pattern where the stitching holes are indicated.

3. Place the poster board patterns for the front and back of the frame on the leather. Begin cutting out the pieces by using a 5/16-inch (8 mm) drive punch to punch the four rounded corners of the window opening. Then use the knife and straightedge to cut the straight edges of the window (photo 1). Use the scratch awl to pierce the position of the stitching holes around the window.

4. On the back of the frame use the knife to cut a ⅜-inch (9.5 mm) slit at the bottom of the flap as indicated on the pattern. Cut a tab for the flap from leather that measures ⁵⁄₁₆ x 1½ inches (8 x 38 mm). If your frame is accompanied by a dowel for propping it, use the ¼-inch (6 mm) drive punch to make a hole along the bottom of the frame for the dowel.

5. To determine the length of leather strap needed to surround the frame, stretch the cloth measuring tape around the outside edge and add ⅛ inch (3 mm) to this measurement. Use the straightedge and knife to cut out a leather strap that is the same thickness as the frame and the length of the measurement you've determined.

6. Use the sponge to case (wet) the leather to be used on the frame's front. Use the straightedge and the fine-tip marker to transfer the guidelines for the front onto the tracing film. Position the film on the front piece, and use the stylus to transfer the lines. Remove the film from the leather.

7. Use the straightedge as a guide for your swivel knife, and carve the lines.

8. Refer to the finished photo on page 64 to guide you in stamping the following patterns on the cased leather front using stamps and a mallet:

a. Stamp the repeat zigzag pattern with the veiner tool.

b. Add the seed to the pattern using the seed tool.

c. With the camouflage tool, stamp an accent around the stamped seed.

d. Using the left side of the second veiner tool, stamp a repeat pattern along the inside curve of the stamped impression that you already made with the other veiner tool.

e. Use the beveler tool to carve along the edge of the carved lines (see page 11), accentuating the carved area of the frame and creating a smooth shadow around the design. Allow the leather to dry completely.

9. Use the ¹⁄₁₆-inch (1.6 mm) drive punch to punch out the stitching holes around the window (photo 2).

10. Use the fine-tip "liner" paintbrush and red acrylic paint to highlight the seed stamp impressions. Allow the paint to dry.

11. Apply leather wax to the leather, and buff it with a soft cloth to achieve a mellow finish. (If any white lines appear after buffing, apply low heat to the area with a blow dryer to loosen the wax. With a horsehair shoe brush, buff the leather surface to remove the wax buildup.)

12. Thread the leather lace onto the two-prong needle. Sew a running stitch through the punched holes on the front leather piece. Leave the loose ends hanging rather than knotting them. (They will be secured after the leather front is cemented into place.)

13. Use a rectangular strip of poster board to spread a layer of contact cement to the underside of the leather frame front as well as the front of the wood frame. Allow the cement to dry slightly and become tacky. Position the leather cover on the frame, and hold it

in place until it is secure. Repeat this process to cement the other leather piece to the back of the frame, avoiding the back flap.

14. To attach the tab to the flap opening, slide the tab ½-inch (1.3 cm) into the slit and secure it to the back of the flap with contact cement. Fold the protruding side of the flap in half, and secure with cement to form a tab.

15. Carefully apply a layer of contact cement to the back of the leather strap that you cut in step 5, then apply cement to the edge of the frame. Allow the cement to become slightly tacky, then press the strap into place around the edge.

16. Place the glass or plastic sheet in the frame opening, followed by a photo or other image and the foamboard (photo 3).

2

3

Tooled Box Set

Use repeating tooled patterns to make turn paper machè boxes into elegant sculptural forms.

MATERIALS AND TOOLS FOR SMALL BOX

Small hexagonal paper machè box with rusted lid (box shown is 3 inches high x 6 inches wide [17.8 x 15.2 cm] and can be purchased at craft stores)

Piece of poster board

4 x 28 -inch (10.2 x 71.1 cm) strip of 7- to 8-ounce (2.78 to 3.18 mm) #1 grade vegetable-tanned leather

1 glass drawer pull with hardware (about 1½ inches [3.8 cm] tall)

2-inch-square x ¾-inch-wide (1.9 cm) block of wood

Geometric stamping tool with spiral or other shape

MATERIALS AND TOOLS FOR TALL BOX

Square paper machè box with rusted lid (box shown is 14 inches high x 5 inches wide [35.6 x 12.7 cm] and can be purchased at craft stores)

Piece of poster board

3 square feet (.27 m²) of 7- to 8- ounce (2.78 to 3.18 mm) #1 grade vegetable tanned leather

1 glass drawer pull with hardware (about 1½ inches [3.8 cm] tall)

2-inch-square x ¾-inch-wide (5.1 cm) block of wood

Stamping tools: geometric, mule foot, camouflage, and seed

3-prong buckstitch lacing (angled) chisel, ⁵⁄₃₂-inch (4 mm)

1-prong buckstitch lacing chisel, ⁵⁄₃₂-inch (4 mm)

⁵⁄₃₂-inch (4 mm) white buckstitch lace

2-prong lacing needle

Leather thimble

Swivel knife

Scratch awl fitted with lacing fib blade

Leather shears

TOOLS AND SUPPLIES FOR BOTH BOXES

Straightedge/ruler

Fine-tip black marker

Craft or "clicker" knife

Sponge

Scratch awl

Marble slab

Empty jar

White and brown acrylic paint

1-inch (2.5 cm) flat paintbrush

Wool scraps

Clear acrylic varnish in spray form

#4 edger

Mallet

Wool scraps

Contact cement

Handheld drill

Screwdriver

3. Use the straightedge and knife to cut out a long rectangular pattern from the poster board that is the width that you derived in step 1 and the length that you derived in step 2.

4. Use a straightedge/ruler and a knife to cut out a piece of leather that is 3 inches (7.6 cm) longer in length and 1 inch (2.5 cm) larger in height than your pattern. (This will allow room for the leather to shrink.)

5. Use a sponge and water to case the leather. Use the scratch awl and the straightedge to mark one horizontal and one vertical guideline that is about ½ inch (1.3 cm) from the edge of the leather strip.

6. Place the marble slab on your work surface. Use the marked guidelines and the spiral stamping tool (see photo 1 for the impression that this tool makes) and mallet to repeatedly stamp the pattern in a diagonal pattern on the cased leather (photo 2). Allow the leather to dry completely.

INSTRUCTIONS FOR SMALL BOX

1. With the box's lid on, use the straightedge to measure the height of the box panel from the bottom of the lid to the base plus twice the thickness of the leather (or about ¼ inch [6 mm]). Jot down this figure.

2. Because the side panels on hexagonal boxes made of paper are often slightly different in size, you'll need to measure the width of all five sides of the box. As you measure each width, use the black marker to write down the exact measurement plus twice the thickness of the leather directly on each box panel. Add together all of the widths that you have recorded on the box.

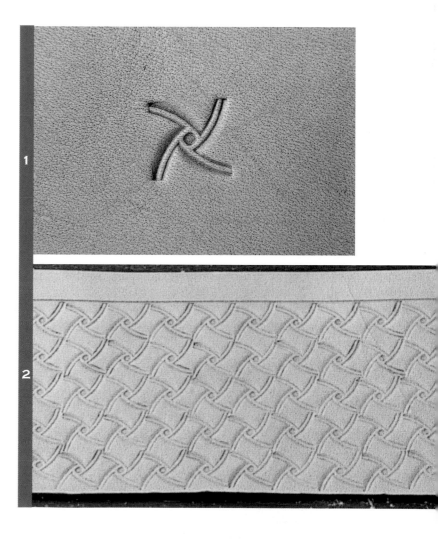

7. In the empty jar, mix five parts of white acrylic paint with two parts of water. Apply a coat of paint with a the 1-inch (2.5 cm) flat paintbrush to a small section at a time, working the paint into the stamped impressions. Use a piece of wool to rub the leather panels lengthwise to remove the excess paint. After the leather has dried, apply a second coat of paint if a whiter finished is desired. Allow the finish to dry completely.

8. Next you'll paint the areas of the paper box that won't be covered with undiluted paint. To do this, remove the lid and paint the sides of the box that lie underneath the lid, plus about ½ inch (1.3 cm). Paint the top edge, and the entire inside of the box. Then paint on a second coat.

9. After the paint dries, flip the box over and paint the bottom of with two coats of white paint. Spray with a coat of varnish.

10. Return to working with the leather. Position the poster board pattern on top of the tooled pattern, and cut the horizontal lines in the leather.

11. To cut each of the panels between the horizontal cuts, cut sequential pieces of leather from the strip that conform to the five width measurements that you marked on the panels of the box. Mark the back of each leather piece with the corresponding measurement.

12. Skive the two vertical (short) edges of each leather panel at a 60° angle with a #4 edger.

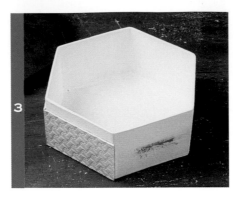

13. Paint the cut edges of all the leather panels with white paint. Once they dry, apply two light coats of spray acrylic leather finish over the entire painted leather surface.

14. To adhere the leather panels, coat the back of the first leather panel and the matching panel on the box with contact cement. Allow the cement to become tacky on both surfaces before positioning the panel. Press the panel into place and hold until secure. Continue this step around the box until all of the panels have been attached (photo 3).

15. Dust off the surface of the lid, and seal it with a coat of spray varnish.

16. Apply two coats of brown paint onto the 2-inch (5.1 cm) square block of wood and seal with spray varnish. Use the handheld drill to drill a hole that is slightly smaller than the size of the drawer pull's screw through the center of the square block of wood. Drill another hole the same size as the screw through the center of the lid. Place the block of wood on the back of the lid, and line up the two drilled holes. Position the drawer pull on the front of the lid, and use the screw-

driver to screw the hardware through the hole in the block into the drawer pull.

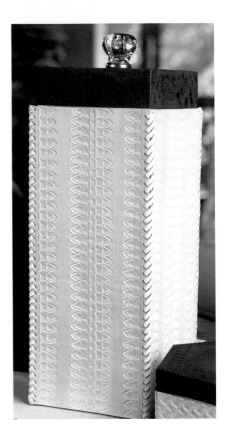

INSTRUCTIONS FOR TALL BOX

1. With the box's lid on, use the straightedge to measure the height of the box panel from the bottom of the lid to the base plus twice the thickness of the leather (or about ¼ inch [6 mm]). Measure the width of the box plus twice the thickness of the leather. Use the knife and straightedge to cut out a poster board pattern using these measurements.

2. On your piece of leather, measure out an area that is four times the width and height that you determined in step 1 plus an inch (2.5 cm) on each side to allow for shrinkage. Mark this area off with the scratch awl and a straightedge.

3. Case the leather with a sponge and water. Use the swivel knife and a straightedge to cut two straight vertical lines spaced ⅛ inch (3 mm) apart every 2¼ inches (5.7 cm) along the length of the piece. (These border lines will be as the axis of your tooled designs.)

4. Place the marble slab on your work surface. On either side of the vertical lines that you cut in step 3, use the geometric stamp to stamp a repeating pattern with about ¼-inch (6 mm) between each stamp. Use the mulefoot stamp to add the arched pattern on either side of the geometric pattern, creating a vertical, symmetrical pattern. Within the mulefoot pattern, add textural impressions with the camouflage stamp.

5. As the final tooling step, skip over the first set of vertical stamped impressions on one end of your leather piece, and, on the second set of impressions, use the seeder stamp to stamp impressions ¼ inch (6 mm) apart down the middle of the central lines to created "beaded borders." Continue to add these impressions to every other set of impressions along the central axis.

6. Allow the leather to dry completely.

7. Refer to steps 7 through 9 for the small hexagonal box, and follow the same steps to paint the finish on the leather. Allow the leather to dry.

8. Use the poster board pattern, knife, and straightedge to cut out four indentical pieces of leather, placing the beaded borders in the center of each panel.

9. Use the three-prong chisel to punch a series of uniform angled/diagonal slits ⅛-inch (3 mm) from each of the long edges of the four pieces. Punch the slits with a three-prong angle chisel, making sure the slits are uniform along each of the side panels.

9. Carefully skive the two vertical edges of leather panels at a 45° angle with the #4 edger. Paint the cut edges of all the leather panels with white paint. Once they dry, apply two light coats of spray acrylic leather finish over the entire painted leather surface.

10. To adhere the leather panels, coat the back of each leather panel and a corresponding panel on the box with contact cement, leaving a 1½-inch (3.8 cm) margin on the sides and bottom, and a ½-inch (1.3 cm) margin on the top. Allow the cement to become tacky on both surfaces before positioning the panel. Press the panel into place and hold until secure. Continue this step around the box until all of the panels have been attached.

11. Multiply the length of one of the side panels by four, and use this measurement to cut off a length of buckstitch lace. Attach the lace to a two-prong needle (photo 4).

12. On the box, begin by lacing from the underside of the leather and out of first slit on left side (if right handed) or the right side (if left handed) on the bottom edge of a box corner. Leave a

½-inch (1.3 cm) tail of lace, and tuck it between the leather and the box.

13. Thread the lace through the slit directly across from the first slit, then thread it back through both slits again to tighten it. Begin threading at a diagonal through the next hole up on the other side, and thread back through the stitch that is directly on the other side. Continue this diagonal whipstitch until you reach the top of the box. End the stitch the same way you began. Repeat this step for the remaining three corners (photo 5).

14. Follow steps 15 and 16 from the small hexagonal box instructions to finish the lid of the box (photo 6).

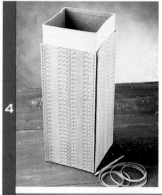

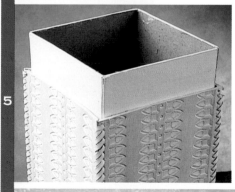

STENCILED WASTEBASKET

THE ELEGANCE OF BLACK LEATHER
COMBINED WITH A REVERSED
STENCIL DESIGN COVERS UP THIS
WASTEBASKET'S TRUE FUNCTION
AS A RECEPTABLE FOR TRASH.

MATERIALS

Tapered unfinished wooden wastebasket with four sides (available from craft stores or unfinished furniture stores)
(Wastebasket shown: front and back panels measure 11 x 14 inches [27.9 x 35.6 cm]; side panels measure 7 x 10 inches [17.8 x 25.4 cm])

2 sheets of poster board

Four $1\frac{1}{2}$-inch-square (3.8 cm) blocks of wood

Water-based wood sealer

Black acrylic paint

Water-based varnish

Black deer-tanned cowhide (we began with 5 square feet [.45 m²] to cover our wastebasket)

Precut decorative stencil of your choice

Stencil paint in contrasting valves (we used light tan and warm brown)

Eight 1-inch (2.5 cm) pewter upholstery tacks

Four #8 $1\frac{3}{4}$-inch (4.4 cm) wood screws

TOOLS AND SUPPLIES

Pencil

2 sheets of poster board

Straightedge/ruler

Brown craft paper

Scissors

Fine-grit sandpaper

$1\frac{1}{2}$-inch (3.8 cm) flat paintbrush

Craft or "clicker" knife

Several sheets of newsprint paper

Contact cement

Sticky notes or low-tack drafting tape

1-inch (2.5 cm) round stencil brush

Paper towels

Needle-nose pliers

Polymer-head mallet or tack hammer

Small handheld drill

#8 countersink drill bit

1. To create templates for your wastebasket, trace the outline of the front and one of the sides onto the poster board. Use the straightedge to draw parallel lines that are 1½ inches (3.8 cm) above the top and bottom of each of the two patterns, and extend the side of the pattern up to meet this line. Cut out the pattern.

2. Trace the poster board patterns onto the brown craft paper, and cut out the shapes with scissors. Fit the brown paper patterns to the front and one side of the wastebasket, making adjustments to the pattern in the 1½-inch (3.8 cm) margins at the top and bottom so that the panels will be mitered at the top and bottom. After you've fitted the brown paper patterns, alter the poster board patterns accordingly (photo 1).

3. Sand the surface and all rough edges of the wastebasket.

4. Use the flat paintbrush to paint the interior and the base of the wastebasket as well as the four wooden blocks with a coat of water-based sealer. Clean the brush with water. Allow all pieces to dry.

5. Apply two coats of black acrylic paint over the sealer as well as the joining edges of each top corner of the wastebasket. Paint the four blocks with two coats of acrylic paint. After the paint dries, apply a final coat of water-based varnish to all painted areas of the pieces.

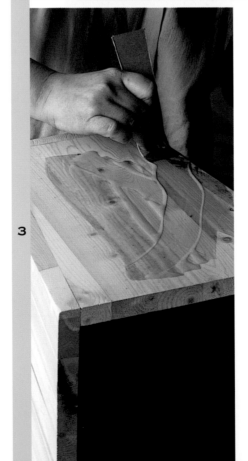

6. Use the knife and the poster board patterns to cut out two panels of black leather for the identical front, back, and sides of the wastebasket.

7. Cover your work surface with newsprint paper. Cut out a couple of rectangular strips from poster board to use as spreaders for the contact cement. Place the leather panels grain side down on the paper. Pour out a portion of contact cement on the back of one of the panels, and spread it out evenly (photo 2). Apply cement on a matching side of the wastebasket and to the bottom, top edge, and inside, where the leather panel will overlap (photo 3).

8. Carefully place the leather panel on the prepared wood surface and press it from the middle out to adhere it (photo 4). Repeat this step with the remaining three leather panels, pressing the leather flaps down inside the wastebasket (photo 5). Allow the panels to dry overnight.

9. Position your stencil along the front or back panel of the wastebasket where you want the design to fall. Hold the edges of the stencil in place with sticky notes or low-tack drafting tape.

10. Load the stencil brush with the lighter-colored paint. Dab any excess paint off on a paper towel. Drybrush the color over the whole stencil area by repeatedly pouncing the brush up and down lightly (photo 6). Repeat this

step with the darker color of paint to create a mottled, light/dark effect.

11. Remove the stencil (photo 7). Use the same process to paint the stencilled pattern on the opposite side of the wastebasket.

12. On the sides of the basket, use sticky notes or drafting tape to mask off a simple diamond shape. Choose a portion of the stencil to use within this framework, and paint on a mottled stenciled design as you did in step

13. Allow the paint to dry for 24 hours.

14. Use the pliers and a polymer mallet or tack hammer to add pewter-colored tacks to the four corners of each diamond shape (photo 8).

15. Mark a center point on one side of each wooden block. Use the drill fitted with the countersink bit to drill a hole at each marked point.

16. Flip the wastebasket over. Place the edges of each block 1½ inches (3.8 cm) from the edges of each corner of the bottom. Use the handheld drill to screw the wood screws all the way through the blocks and into the bottom of the wastebasket (photo 9).

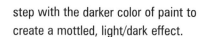

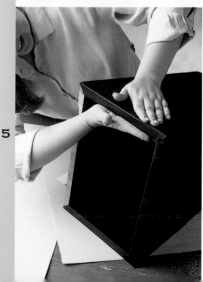

Stamped Patchwork Pillows

THESE VIBRANT, COLORFUL PILLOWS MADE OF SOFT SUEDE PIECES STAMPED WITH METALLIC DESIGNS LEND NEW MEANING TO SEWN PATCHWORK.

MATERIALS FOR TWO PILLOWS

8 square feet (.72 m²) of black pig suede

Black polyester thread

1 square foot (.09 m²) of pig suede in each of the following colors: medium brown, red, rust, purple

Rubber stamps of your choice

Water-based fabric or acrylic paint in each of the following colors: black, metallic silver, metallic bronze, metallic copper

8 small plain buttons or stays (for the underside of the pillow)

8 round decorative buttons (for the front of the pillow)

Pillow forms: 14 x 14 inch (35.6 x 35.6 cm), 14 x 18 inch (35.6 x 45.7 cm)

TOOLS AND SUPPLIES

Cutting mat

Craft knife or "clicker" knife

Straightedge/ruler

White chalk pencil

Sewing machine fitted with size 14 leather needle (or needle appropriate for your machine)

Rubber cement

1½-inch-wide (3.8 cm) metal brayer (roller)

Wedge-shaped cosmetic sponges

Stamp cleaner (optional)

Fine-tip "liner" paintbrush

Small binder clips

Glover's needle

1. Place the cutting mat on your work surface. For pillow backings, use the knife to cut the following: one 15 x 15-inch (38.1 x 38.1 cm) piece of black suede and one 15 x 19-inch (38.1 x 48.3 cm) piece of black suede.

2. For the border of the square pillow, cut four 3 x 15-inch (7.6 x 38.1 cm) black suede strips. For the rectangular pillow, cut two 3 x 15-inch (7.6 x 38.1 cm) black suede strips and two 3 x 19-inch (7.6 x 48.3 cm) black suede strips.

3. Position all of the strips right side down on your work surface. Fold the ends of each strip over at a 45° angle, and use the chalk and straightedge to mark where the fold lies. Trim the suede ½ inch (1.3 cm) from this line (leaving room for a seam allowance).

4. Use the straightedge and chalk to mark a line on the black strips that is ½ inch (1.3 cm) from each of the shorter inside edges.

5. Use the sewing machine threaded with black thread to sew together the four 3 x 15-inch (7.6 x 38.1 cm) mitered strips with right sides together along the fold lines that you marked in step 3, stopping at the point where the fold line crosses the white line you drew in step 4.

6. Cut the thread, and knot the loose ends on either side of the seam. Press open the seam allowances with your fingers, and secure them with rubber cement and the metal brayer.

7. Repeat steps 4 through 6 to sew together the border strips for the rectangular pillow.

8. For the front of the square pillow, cut one 4-inch (10.2 cm) square from each of the following suedes: red, medium brown, and rust. Cut one 4 x 7-inch (10.2 x 17.8 cm) piece from each of the following suedes: rust, purple, and red. Place these pieces in a pile.

9. For the front of the rectangular pillow, cut one 4 x 4-inch (10.2 x 10.2 cm) piece from each of the following suedes: red, medium brown, rust, and purple. Cut one 4 x 7-inch (10.2 x 17.8 cm) piece from each of the following suedes: rust, purple, red, and medium brown. Place these pieces in a pile.

10. Stamp the suede pieces for the square pillow first. To do this, apply an even coat of paint to the stamp of your choice with a cosmetic sponge. Position the stamp on the front of the suede piece, and apply even pressure. Carefully lift the stamp straight up to remove it. Add more paint and reuse the stamp as you wish. When finished, clean the stamp immediately with stamp cleaner, or wash clean with soap and water.

11. Continue stamping the pieces until you are satisfied with your design (photo 1). Use the fine-tip "liner" brush to add additional detail and color to the stamped designs. Allow the paint to dry completely.

1

12. Stamp the pieces for the rectangular pillow, and set them aside to dry.

13. After they dry, position the stamped pieces for the square pillow in the configuration seen in the project photo on page 76. Machine stitch each of the pieces together in a patchwork fashion with a $\frac{1}{2}$-inch (1.3 cm) seam allowance. Press out and glue all the seam allowances with rubber cement, smoothing then out with the metal brayer. Assemble the pieces for the rectangular pillow in the same fashion.

14. To attach the black mitered edging to the square pillow front, place the right sides of the two pieces together, and hold the edges in place with small binder clips. Sew together with a $\frac{1}{2}$-inch (1.3 cm) seam. Press out the seams and glue them in place with rubber cement before smoothing them out with the metal brayer. Repeat these steps to sew the mitered black edging to the rectangular pillow front.

15. Thread the glover's needle with a single strand of black thread. Place one of the small plain buttons on the backside of the square pillow front at the corner, and pull the thread up through the button to the front.

16. Thread a round decorative button onto the thread from the front, and push the needle back down through the plain button on the other side. Secure the thread by passing back to the front button again, then back down through the plain button. Secure the

thread with several overhand knots. Add buttons to the remaining three corners of the square pillow and the corners of the rectangular pillow (photo 2).

17. Place the pillow fronts and backs right sides together, and hold them together with binder clips. Machine stitch three of the four edges of each pillow with a $\frac{1}{2}$-inch (1.3 cm) seam allowance. Press open the seam allowances, glue them down with rubber cement, and roll out the seams with the metal brayer.

18. Turn both of the pillow covers right side out. Insert the pillow forms, and use the appliqué needle and black thread to hand stitch the open edge closed with a blind stitch.

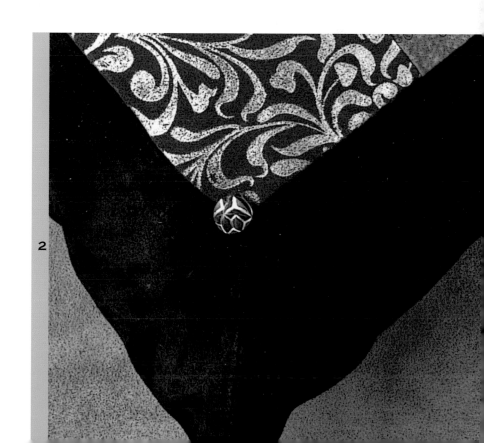

2

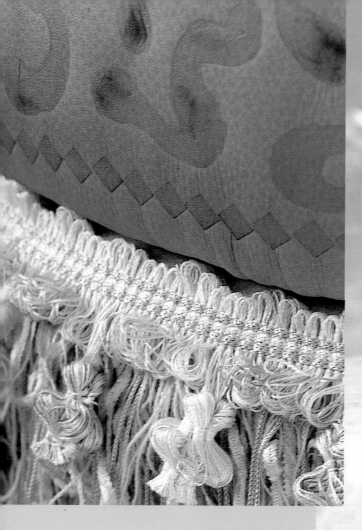

BRANDED FOOTSTOOL

WITH SIMPLE UPHOLSTERY TECHNIQUES YOU CAN ASSEMBLE THIS EXOTIC-LOOKING FOOTSTOOL. THE UNUSUAL BRANDED DESIGNS ARE MADE WITH A COMMON WOODBURNING TOOL.

MATERIALS

15 square feet (1.35 m²) gold-colored deerskin

3 x 18-inch (7.6 x 45.7 cm) round piece of firm foam padding (available at fabric and upholstery stores)

2 round wooden boards ("rounders"), 1¼ x 18 inches (3.2 x 45.7 cm) in diameter (available at hardware or home supply stores)

Quilt batting, 35 x 52-inch (88.9 x 132.1 cm) piece

4 metal top plates with screws (available at hardware or home supply stores)

Several #6 1½-inch (3.8 cm) wood screws

Gold thread

4 turned-wood furniture legs, 9 x 2½-inch (22.9 x 6.4 cm) diameter (available at home supply stores)

Wood sealer

Gray acrylic paint

Antique stain

Satin varnish

58-inch-long (147.3 cm) piece of 5-inch-wide (12.7 cm) decorative fringe (optional)

TOOLS AND SUPPLIES

Fine-tip black marker

Ball of string

Fabric scissors

Craft or "clicker" knife

Contact cement

Staple gun and staples

Leather shears

Woodburning tool with square and wedge-shaped grading tip (available at craft supply stores)

Fine-grit sandpaper

Straightedge/ruler

Pencil

Small handheld drill

Screwdriver

Sewing machine fitted with size 16 leather needle (or needle appropriate for your machine)

Medium-sized flat paintbrush (for applying sealer)

Rag (old T-shirt or soft cotton cloth)

INSTRUCTIONS

1. Tie the fine-tip marker to the end of a piece of string that is about 20 inches (50.8 cm) long, and trim the string to a length of about 16½ inches (41.9 cm) long. Scribe a 33-inch (83.8 cm) circle on the piece of deerskin by using the string and marker as a compass. Use the knife to cut out this circular piece of deerskin, as well as two 5 x 28-inch (12.7 x 71.1 cm) pieces of deerskin.

2. Use contact cement to glue the round foam cushion to one of the round wooden boards.

3. Cut out a circular piece of batting that is 31 inches (78.7 cm) in diameter and another piece that is 4 x 54 inches (10.2 x 137.2 cm).

4. Center the round foam cushion facedown on the circular piece of batting. Pull the batting up over the edge at several points on opposite sides of the wooden rounder, stapling the batting in place as you go. Continue to pull up the batting and staple it until it is in place all the way around. Cut away the excess batting, leaving about a 1-inch (2.5 cm) margin of batting.

5. Place the circular piece of deerskin facedown on the work surface, and center the face of the batting-covered cushion on it. Pull the deerskin up over two edges on opposite sides of the wooden backing, and staple the leather in place on either side, about 2 inches

(5.1 cm) from the edge. Staple down two more points opposite one another so that the deerskin is pulled up at four points spaced somewhat evenly apart. Continue to pull up the deerskin on one side and then the other so that it fits around the form smoothly and evenly. Once the deerskin has been secured, use the leather shears to trim it about 1 inch (2.5 cm) from the staples, removing the excess bulk (photo 1).

6. Attach the square tip to the woodburning tool. Heat up the tool. Practice using the tool to brand a scrap of the deerskin. When satisfied with your ability to use the tool, brand a square decorative border along the bottom edge of the deerskin cushion. Allow the tool to cool, and remove the square tip.

7. Attach the grading tip to the woodburning tool. Heat up the tool again. Practice branding full, wavy bands of decoration on a scrap of the deerskin by pressing and rolling the tip along the surface. Clean the tip of the tool with sandpaper as you go along. You'll find that shades of gray are produced by varying the pressure and the time that the tool is held down. Once you're satisfied with your ability to create the design, brand the stool's surface with a random pattern (photo 2).

8. Place the remaining round wooden board (which will become the base of the footstool) on your work surface. Find the center of the board, and then use the straightedge and a pencil to mark the edge of the board at each quarter point. Place each top plate 1

inch (2.5 cm) from the edge at one of the quarter marks. Make a pencil mark in the center indicating where to drill the hole for attaching the plate. Predrill the holes with the handheld drill. Use the screwdriver to attach the top plates with the accompanying screws.

9. Stretch, wrap, and staple the 4 x 54-inch (10.2 x 137.2 cm) length of batting around the wooden base, overlapping the edges on the top and bottom of the board.

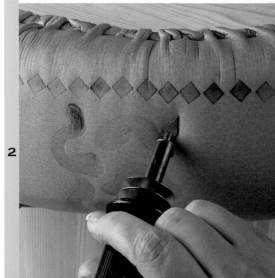

10. Use the sewing machine to sew together the ends of the 5 x 28-inch (12.7 x 71.1 cm) strips of deerskin with a ½-inch (1.3 cm) seam to create a circular piece that fits around the base of the stool. Slide the deerskin piece over the edge of the base with the sewn seam inside (photo 3). Secure it with staples along the top and the bottom. Use leather shears to neatly cut away the excess leather.

11. Place the footstool cushion upside down. Center the footstool base on the cushion with the metal top plates exposed. Secure the base to the cushion with several 1½-inch (3.8 cm) wood screws.

12. Use the paintbrush to apply a coat of wood sealer to the wooden legs, and allow it to dry. Sand the legs lightly, then paint on two coats of gray acrylic paint. After the paint has dried, use the rag to rub on a coat of antique stain. Paint on a coat of satin varnish.

13. Screw the wooden legs to the top plates (photo 4). Adjust the legs until the footstool rests level.

14. If you want to add decorative fringe, use contact cement to attach the fringe around the upholstered edge of the base (photo 5).

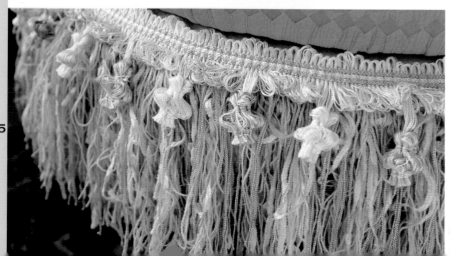

Appliquéd Suede Throw

Make any couch, chair, or bed more enticing with this irresistable brown suede throw backed with red velvet and adorned with appliquéd stamped fans.

Materials

26 square feet (2.3 m²) of dark reddish-brown pig suede

Fan patterns (see page 133)

Piece of poster board

1 square foot (.09 m²) of red pig suede

2 square feet (.18 m²) of gold pig suede

Rubber stamp with fan image

Tri-color pigment stamp pad with metallic colors: black, brown, and beige

Upholstery/nylon threads: red, gold, and brown

1 yard (.9 m) of interfacing for light knits

2 yards (.18 m) of red velvet

Clear nylon thread

30 amber ring-shaped (annular) beads (5 mm)

30 red seed beads (size 11)

Tools and Supplies

Long straightedge/ruler

Craft or "clicker" knife

Glue stick

Fine-tip black marker

Punch board

Teardrop-shaped drive punch

Polymer-head or rawhide mallet

Pie-shaped drive punch

Rubber cement

Sewing machine fitted with size 14 leather needle (or needle appropriate for your machine)

Rotary cutter

Cutting mat

Clothes iron

Pressing cloth or a thick pillowcase

Fabric scissors

Small binder clips

1½-inch-wide (3.8 cm) metal brayer (roller)

Glover's needle

White chalk pencil

Sharp beading needle

Nylon thread

INSTRUCTIONS

1. Use the straightedge and knife to cut the following from the dark reddish-brown suede:
*1 panel that measures 21 x 41 inches (53.3 x 104.1 cm)
*2 panels that measure 25 x 41 inches (63.5 x 104.1 cm) each.

2. Use the glue stick to adhere the two fan patterns to the poster board. Use the knife to cut the patterns out.

3. Place the small fan pattern onto the red suede, and use the knife to cut out 10 pieces. Use the large fan pattern to cut out 10 pieces from the gold suede.

4. Position the fan-shaped stamp on the surface of the tri-color stamp pad with the black portion of the pad at the top of the fan shape. Thoroughly ink the stamp. Stamp the fan image onto the red suede fans, reinking as needed. (See photo 1 showing one small red fan that has been cut out from its pattern and is ready to be stamped.) Allow the ink to dry completely before handling the suede.

5. Place the red fans on the punch board. Use the teardrop punch and mallet to punch a series of holes along the top edge of each of the stamped fan shapes (photo 2). Use the pie-shaped punch to make a single hole right beneath the bottom of the stamped fan shape.

6. Apply an even coat of rubber cement to the back of each red fan and adhere each to a gold suede fan, allowing it to become tacky before sewing.

7. Thread the sewing machine with red thread, and stitch just inside the edge of all of the red fan shapes to hold them in place.

8. On both of the larger dark brown suede panels along the longer 41-inch (104.1 cm) side, position five of the appliquéd fans 2 inches (5.1 cm) from the edge and sides and about 3¼ inches (8.3 cm) apart. Use rubber cement to baste the fans to the suede. Use gold thread to machine stitch around the outside edges to hold them in place.

9. Lay out the 21 x 41-inch (53.3 x 104.1 cm) piece of dark brown suede lengthwise between the unadorned edges of the two appliquéd pieces. Use brown thread to machine stitch a mock flat-fell seam (see page 22) to sew up the two long seams that hold the face of the throw together.

10. Stretch the interfacing in either direction to determine which is less stretchy. Use the straightedge, rotary cutter, and mat to cut seven 3¾ x 36-inch (9.5 x 91.4 cm) strips of interfacing that run in the direction that stretches less.

11. On the backside of the face of the throw, place the strips of interfacing along the edges (photo 3). Heat the clothes iron to the temperature indicated by the manufacturer for bonding the interfacing. Cover the interfacing with the pressing cloth or thick pillowcase to protect the suede from scorching while ironing the interfacing.

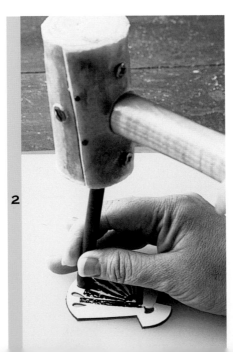

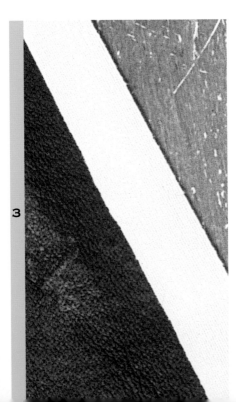

12. Use the fabric scissors to cut out a 41 x 71-inch (104.1 x 180.3 cm) piece of red velvet. Place the right sides of the velvet and suede together, matching the edges all the way around. Hold the edges in place with the binder clips.

13. Machine stitch a ½-inch (1.3 cm) seam along both 41-inch (104.1 cm) ends of the panels, removing the clips as you sew. Repeat this step for one of the 71-inch (180.3 cm) edges, leaving the other edge open.

14. Beginning at one corner of the unsewn edge, sew a seam that is 30 inches (76.2 cm) long, and stop. Beginning at the other corner of the open edge, sew another 30-inch (76.2 cm) seam, and stop, leaving an opening for turning the throw.

15. Before turning the throw, finger press the seams open, and use rubber cement and the metal brayer to baste the seam allowances open.

16. Turn the throw right side out through the open edge. Thread the glover's needle with nylon thread, and hand stitch the seam closed with a blind stitch.

17. Lay out the throw on a flat work surface (such as the floor or a bed) and smooth out any wrinkles. Use a straightedge and chalk pencil to mark a series of dots both horizontally and vertically, where you'll sew through the suede and velvet and attach beads to "quilt" the layers together. (We spaced the beads on our throw about 8 inches [20.3 cm] apart both vertically and horizontally, alternating the place-

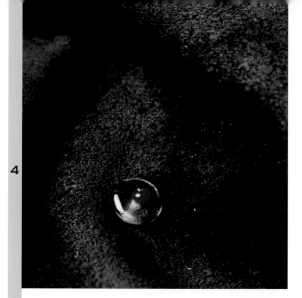

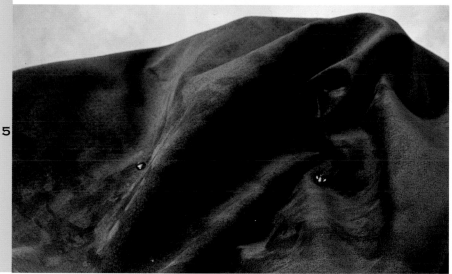

ment of them in each row. You can add more beads than this if you want to create a more complex pattern.)

18. Thread the sharp beading needle with about 12 inches (30.5 cm) of the nylon thread. Reference one of the dots, and pull the threaded needle through the back (velvet) to the front (suede), leaving about a 4-inch (10.2 cm) length of thread hanging on the back that will be secured after you finish beading.

19. Thread on an amber bead followed by a red seed bead. Skipping over the red seed bead, thread the needle back through the amber bead and through the suede and velvet (photo 4). Pull the thread tight, and remove the needle.

20. Tie several square knots in the thread close to the velvet to secure the beads. Repeat this step at the remaining marked locations for beading (photo 5).

STENCILED FRAME WITH MIRROR

HANG YOUR HAT ON THIS EYE-CATCHING FRAMED MIRROR. SHINY BRASS TACKS ON LEATHER ACCENT A SYMMETRICAL DESIGN THAT DRAPES GRACEFULLY AROUND THE MIRROR'S EDGES.

MATERIALS

Frame pattern (see page 133)

4-foot-square (.36 m²) piece of ¾-inch (1.9 cm) plywood

Quilt batting, 35 x 52-inch (88.9 x 132.1 cm) piece

15 square feet (1.3 m²) of tan-colored deer-tanned cowhide

Purchased stencil of your choice

Stencil paints (we used medium brown, dark brown, yellow ochre, dark red, gray-green, and bright yellow)

Spray acrylic leather finish

Antique brass upholstery tacks

13 x 25-inch (33 x 63.5 cm) mirror

Package of mirror hardware (for attaching mirror to back of frame)

Picture-hanging hardware made for heavy frame

2 antique brass hat hooks with fitting flat-head woodscrews

1½ yards (3.8 cm) black lining upholstery fabric

TOOLS AND SUPPLIES

Black fine-tip marker

Jigsaw/scroll saw

Medium-grit sandpaper

Leather shears

Staple gun and staples

Craft or "clicker" knife

Pad of sticky notes or roll of low-tack adhesive tape

Stencil brushes

Needle-nosed pliers

Polymer-head mallet or tack hammer

Screwdriver

⅛-inch (3 mm) round hole drive punch

Punch board

Hand-held drill

INSTRUCTIONS

1. Use the fine-tip marker to trace the frame pattern onto the piece of plywood. Use the jigsaw to cut out the frame, including the window opening. Use the sandpaper to sand away any rough edges and splinters on the surface of the wood and inside the window.

Note: For the next steps, you may need a friend or family member to assist you.

2. Lay out the batting on your work surface, and center the plywood frame facedown on it. Use shears to trim the batting, leaving a 3-inch (7.6 cm) margin around the frame. Wrap the batting around the frame's edges to the backside, and staple it in place. Use the shears to cut away any excess batting.

3. Position the piece of leather grain side down on your work surface. Position the face of the frame on the leather, leaving a margin of approximately 6 inches (15.2 cm) around the edge of the frame as you cut away the excess leather with the knife.

4. Beginning with the notched and inwardly curved areas of the frame, stretch the leather to the back of the frame on opposite sides, and staple it in place. Pull the leather taut as you go. Trim away the excess leather as you go (photo 1). Clip the edges of the leather where it needed so that you can flatten it as you staple it (photo 2). (This is where that extra pair of hands can come in handy!)

5. Mark an 8 x 20-inch (20.3 x 50.8 cm) rectangle inside the window opening on the back side of the leather, leaving a 4-inch (10.2 cm) margin of leather inside the frame opening. Use the knife to cut along the lines to reveal the opening, and remove the rectangular piece of leather. Then cut diagonal slits in the leather to within 1 inch (2.5 cm) of the corners of the underlying frame's window. You'll end up with four hanging flaps of leather.

6. Stretch a corner of one of the leather flaps to the backside of the frame, and staple it in place. Staple the other corner of the flap on the back, pulling the length of the flap tightly between the two corners. Staple the length on the back. Repeat this process on the opposite side of the window, followed by the two remaining flaps. Use the shears to neatly trim off the excess leather (photo 3).

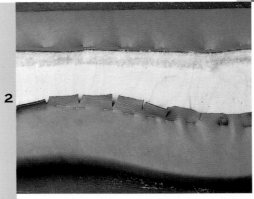

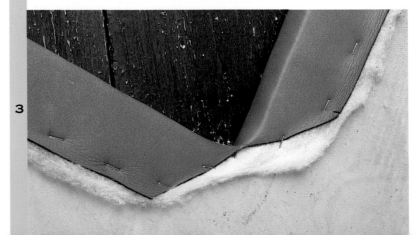

7. Cut a piece of black lining fabric that is slightly larger than the frame. Fold the outer edges of the fabric under, and staple it on the back of the frame around the edges. Cut out an opening in the fabric for the window, fold the edges of the fabric under, and staple it close to the edge of the window opening.

8. Carefully position the stencil pattern on the front of the leather frame, and lightly secure it with sticky notes or low-tack adhesive tape. (If you're using a series of overlapping stencils, position the first stencil, and use the scratch awl to mark the position of the registration marks with a small puncture mark [photo 4]. Follow with subsequent stencils.) Use the stencil paints and brush to paint on the designs.

9. Have your helper hold the frame upright so you can access the inside edge of the frame's window. Use the needle-nose pliers to hold one of the uphostery tacks in a vertical position at one corner of the lowest edge of the frame. Tap the tack into place with the polymer-head mallet or tack hammer. Continue to affix tacks side by side around the inside of the frame's opening until you've gone all the way around.

10. Place the frame flat on your work surface. Continue to add decorative upholstery tacks to the front of the mirror frame in a design of your choice (photo 5).

11. Position the mirror on the backside of the frame within the window opening. Use the screwdriver to attach the mirror hardware to the back of the frame. Attach the picture-hanging hardware to the back as well (photo 6).

12. On the front of the frame, position the two hat hooks on either side of the frame, equidistant from the edges, and make a dot to indicate the position of each with the black marker. To prevent damage to the leather or batting, use the ⅛-inch (3 mm) drive punch to perforate the leather and batting at these points. Use the hand-held drill to predrill each of the screw holes in the exposed wood (photo 7). Use the screwdriver and flat-head screws to attach the hooks.

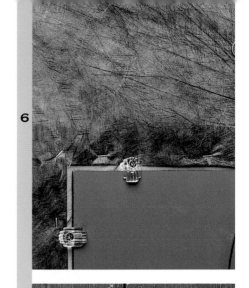

6

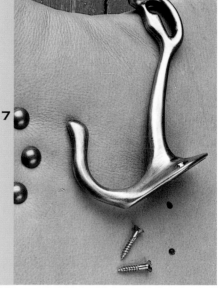

7

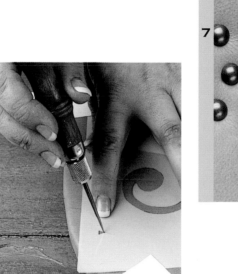

4

5

PHOTO TRANSFER PILLOWS

TRANSFER YOUR FAVORITE FAMILY PHOTOS TO DEERSKIN, AND FRAME THEM IN OVAL WINDOWS STUDDED WITH PARACHUTE SPOTS. THESE PILLOWS ARE CERTAIN TO BECOME HEIRLOOMS!

MATERIALS FOR ONE PILLOW

Oval template (see page 134)

Family photo

Photo transfer paper (available at craft supply stores, copy centers)

1 square foot (.09 m²) smoke-colored deerskin

Newsprint paper

Double thickness mat board

2 pieces of poster board

4 square feet (.36 m²) of deer-tanned cowhide in tan color

Upholstery/nylon thread to match deer-tanned cowhide

⅜-inch (9.5 mm) parachute spots (box of 100)

34-inch (86.4 cm) length of gold-colored deer-tanned fringe (or follow instructions on page 24 to make your own fringe from a piece of smoke-colored deerskin)

16 x 16-inch (40.6 x 40.6 cm) pillow form

Gray upholstery/nylon thread

TOOLS AND SUPPLIES

Craft or "clicker" knife

Straightedge/ruler

Clothes iron

Black fine-tip marker

Rubber cement

Tools and Supplies continued on next page

Sewing machine fitted with size 16 leather needle (or needle appropriate for your machine)

³⁄₃₂-inch (2.4 mm) lacing chisel

Mallet

Punch board

³⁄₁₆-inch (4.8 mm) round hole drive punch

the transferred image facedown on it. Cover the top with a sheet of newsprint paper.

4. Press the heated iron firmly over the surface of the newsprint for the amount of time recommended by the manufacturer of the transfer paper. Remove the newsprint, and quickly peel off the paper backing to reveal the image on the leather.

5. From a piece of poster board, use the craft knife to cut out the following patterns for the pillow cover:
*Pillow front (using template as guide):
   17 x 17-inch (43.2 x 43.2 cm) piece
   with a 6½ x 8½-inch (16.5 x 21.6 cm)
   oval window
*Envelope pillow backing pieces:
   8½ x 17-inch (21.6 x 43.2 cm) pattern
   10 x 17-inch (25.4 x 43.2 cm) pattern

6. Next, cut out a poster board piece for positioning ³⁄₁₆-inch (4.8 mm) holes along the envelope opening for lacing. To do this, cut out a 4 x 17-inch (10.2 x 43.2 cm) piece of poster board. Use the straightedge and marker to draw a line through the center of the length of the board. Mark pairs of dots spaced ³⁄₈ inch (9.5 mm) on either side of the centerline and ¾ inch (1.9 cm) apart.

7. Place the patterns for the pillow cover on the deer-tanned cowhide, and use the knife to cut out the pillow front and two pillow back pieces for each pillow form.

8. To assemble the pillow front, begin by placing the deerskin with the photo transfer behind the oval window of the leather pillow front (photo 1). Use rubber cement to baste the deerskin in place about ¼ inch (6 mm) from the edge of the oval window. Use the sewing machine and gray thread to

INSTRUCTIONS

1. Use a photocopy machine to reduce or enlarge your photo to fit inside the oval template. Transfer the image onto the transfer paper, following the manufacturer's instructions.

2. Use your knife to cut a piece of smoke-colored deerskin that is about 2 inches (5.1 cm) larger all the way around than the transferred image.

3. Use the straightedge and knife to cut a piece of double thickness mat board that is 5 inches (12.7 cm) larger on all sides than the piece of smoke-colored deerskin. Heat the iron to the highest no-steam setting. Center the deerskin faceup on the mat board with

1

topstitch about ¼ inch (6 mm) from the edge of the window. On the back of the pillow front, trim away the excess deerskin, leaving a narrow seam allowance.

9. To frame the photo with parachute spots, make marks with the prongs of the spots around the oval frame, ⅛ inch (3 mm) from the topstitching and ¼ inch (6 mm) apart. Using the prong impressions as a guide, make small incisions with the lacing chisel and mallet before pushing the spots through the leather (photo 2). From the backside of the leather, use the end of the chisel to fold the spot prongs down so they are locked into place (photo 3).

10. Use the knife to cut two 17-inch (43.2 cm) lengths of gold deer-tanned fringe. (To add a twisted appearance to the fringe, follow the instructions on page 25.)

11. Lay the smaller pillow back piece over the larger one, lining up the edges to form a 17-inch (43.2 cm) square pillow back. Baste the joining outer edges together with rubber cement.

12. Place the punch board on your work surface. Line up the centerline of the pattern that you cut in step 6 with the line formed by the overlap of the two back pieces. Use the ³⁄₁₆-inch (4.8 mm) drive punch and mallet to punch holes through both thicknesses of leather along the envelope opening.

13. To assemble the pillow cover, place the right sides of the pillow front

and back together. Baste them together along the edges with rubber cement.

14. Use gray thread to machine stitch the back and front of the pillow together with a ½-inch (1.3 cm) seam allowance. Turn the pillow cover right side out through the open slit. Insert the pillow form into the pillow cover.

15. Use the knife to cut a 32-inch (81.3 cm) length of leather thong from the deer-tanned cowhide. Attach each of the lace ends to one of the threaded lacing needles. From inside the pillow cover, thread each needle through one hole along the bottom edge of the envelope opening on opposite sides. Cross one thong over the other and place each needle into the next hole across from the exiting hole (photo 4). Lace up the pillow opening with this stitch, and tie together the ends of the lace with a knot. Hide the knot and excess lace ends inside the pillow cover.

3

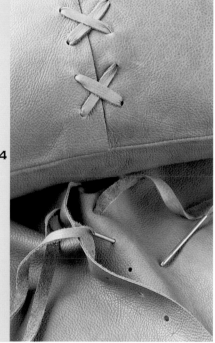

4

2

PILLOW SET WITH
STAMPED AND PERFORATED SLEEVES

SLICK SILK FABRICS CONTRAST WITH SOFT LUSH SUEDES ON THESE GORGEOUS
PILLOWS. THE SUEDE SLEEVES ARE STAMPED WITH DESIGNS AND PERFORATED
TO REVEAL GLIMMERS OF FABRIC UNDERNEATH.

MATERIALS

1 yard (.9 m) each of bright green and purple silk

22 x 18-inch (55.9 x 45.7 cm) pillow form

20-inch-long x 9-inch-diameter (50.8 x 22.9 cm) bolster pillow form

4 square feet (.36 m²) each of bright green and purple pig suede

Polyester threads to match silk and suede

Rubber stamps

Acrylic or fabric paint in the following colors: pearl violet, metallic olive green, metallic bronze, copper, black

Stamp cleaner (optional)

4 yards (3.6 m) of black feather fringe or other fringe of your choice

TOOLS AND SUPPLIES

Fabric scissors

Cloth tape measure

Craft or "clicker" knife

Clothes iron

Straight pins

Sewing machine

Sharp sewing needle for hand stitching silk

Wedge-shaped cosmetic sponges

Decorative punches (we used moon, pie, diamond, and teardrop shapes)

Round drive punches (we used ³⁄₁₆-inch [4.8 mm] and ⁵⁄₁₆-inch [8 mm])

Punch board

Mallet

Straightedge/ruler

Rotary cutter with wave blade

Tools and Supplies continued on next page

Cutting mat

Water-based white leather adhesive

Size 14 leather needle (or needle appropriate for your machine)

Binder clips

Rubber cement

1½-inch-wide (3.8 cm) metal brayer (roller)

INSTRUCTIONS

1. For covering the rectangular pillow form, use fabric scissors to cut a 24 x 38-inch (61 x 96.5 cm) piece of green silk. Use the knife to cut a purple piece of suede for the sleeve that measures 11 x 38 inches (27.9 x 96.5 cm).

2. For covering the round bolster form, cut one 21 x 29-inch (53.3 x 73.7 cm) piece of purple silk and two 10-inch (25.4 cm) round pieces of purple silk. Use the knife to cut a green piece of suede for the sleeve that measures 12 x 29 inches (53.5 x 73.7 cm).

3. Fold the length of green silk in half, right sides together, and pin the ends together. Thread the sewing machine with green thread, and sew a ½-inch-wide (1.3 cm) seam 6 inches (15.2 cm) from either end, leaving the middle section unsewn.

4. Press open the seam, and center it along the length of the silk (so that you have a rectangular shape with an opening in it). Pin the sides together, and sew them up with a ½-inch (1.3 cm) seam. Turn the pillow cover right side out (photo 1), and slide the rectangular pillow inside through the opening. Blind stitch the opening closed with green thread and the sharp needle.

5. Fold the length of the purple silk in half, right sides together, and pin the ends together. Thread the machine

with purple thread, and sew a ½-inch-wide (1.3 cm) seam 6 inches (15.2 cm) from either end, leaving the middle section unsewn. With right sides together, pin each of the remaining round pieces of purple silk to the open ends of the bolster cover. Machine stitch the pieces together with a ½-inch (1.3 cm) seam. Iron the seams open. Turn the pillow cover right side out, and slide in the pillow through the opening. Blind stitch the opening closed with purple thread and a sharp needle.

6. To create colorful stamped designs on the front of the suede pieces, apply an even coat of paint to the stamp of your choice with a cosmetic sponge. Position the stamp on the front of the suede piece, and apply even pressure. Carefully lift the stamp straight up to remove it. Add more paint and reuse the stamp as you wish. When finished, clean the stamp immediately with stamp cleaner, or wash clean with soap and water before applying another color. Continue this process to add more stamped designs in various colors until you are satisfied with the way the suede covers look (photo 2). Allow the paint to dry completely.

3

7. Place the punch board on your work surface. Using the stamp images as a guide, punch decorative patterns on the suede's surface with a variety of round and decorative punches and the mallet.

8. Place one of the suede pieces face-up on the cutting mat. Place the straightedge along one of the long sides of it about $\frac{1}{4}$ inch (6 mm) from the edge. Use the rotary cutter fitted with a wave blade to cut a decorative edge along the long edge (photo 3). Repeat on the other side of the piece. Cut the long edges of the second suede piece in the same fashion.

4

9. Cut four lengths of fringe that match each of the long sides of the two pieces of suede. Use the white leather adhesive to glue the fringe underneath each of the cut edges. Weigh down the edges on top, and allow to dry thoroughly.

10. After the glue is dry, use the sewing machine fitted with the leather needle to machine stitch the fringe to the suede's edge with a $\frac{1}{2}$-inch (1.3 cm) seam allowance.

11. Fold the lengths of the suede pieces in half with the right sides together. Use binder clips to temporarily secure the ends. Machine stitch the ends of the suede together with a $\frac{1}{2}$-inch (1.3 cm) seam allowance. Press open the seams, glue them down with rubber cement, and roll them out with the metal brayer.

12. Turn the suede pillow sleeves right side out and slide them gently onto the pillows, being careful not to harm the fringe (photo 4).

STAMPED OTTOMAN

THIS GENEROUSLY PADDED
OTTOMAN LENDS DIGNITY TO ANY
ROOM, WHILE PROVIDING A
MOVEABLE PLACE TO LOUNGE.
STAMPED DESIGNS ACCENTED WITH
BRASS TACKS COMPLIMENT ITS
HORIZONTAL DESIGN.

MATERIALS

2 pieces of pine wood, each 1 x 8 x 16 inches
(2.5 x 20.3 x 40.6 cm)

2 pieces of pine wood, each 1 x 8 x 24 inches
(2.5 x 20.3 x 61 cm)

2 pieces of plywood, each $\frac{3}{4}$ x 18 x 24 inches
(1.9 x 45.7 x 61 cm)

#8 1$\frac{3}{4}$-inch (4.4 cm) wood screws

Pine post/rail cut to the following:

  2 lengths, each 1$\frac{1}{2}$ x 1$\frac{1}{2}$ x 15$\frac{1}{4}$ inches
  (3.8 x 3.8 x 38.7 cm)

  2 lengths, each 1$\frac{1}{2}$ x 1$\frac{1}{2}$ x 21$\frac{1}{4}$ inches
  (3.8 x 3.8 x 54 cm)

6-inch-thick (15.2 cm) firm foam padding, cut to
18 x 24 inches (45.7 x 61 cm)

Quilt batting, 36 x 42 inches (91.4 x 106.7 cm)

22 square feet (1.98 m^2) of tan-colored deer-tanned cowhide

Fabric paints: black and metallic bronze

4-inch-square (26 cm^2) rubber stamp with
design of your choice

Upholstery or nylon thread
to match cowhide

14 brass upholstery tacks,
each $\frac{5}{8}$-inch (1.6 cm) wide

Nine #6 1$\frac{5}{8}$-inch (4.1 cm) rough-thread
deck screws

4 heavy-duty top plates with hardware
(screws)

18 x 24-inch (45.7 x 61 cm) piece of black
upholstery lining fabric

4 square wooden furniture feet

TOOLS AND SUPPLIES

Small handheld drill

Screwdriver

Rubber cement

Staple gun and staples

Fabric scissors

Leather shears

Craft or "clicker" knife

Straightedge/ruler

3 x 5-inch (7.6 x 12.7 cm) sticky notepad

Piece of glass, old ceramic plate, or other slick surface to use as a palette

4-inch-wide (10.2 cm) rubber brayer

Fine-tip "liner" paintbrush

Sewing machine equipped with size 16 leather needle (or needle appropriate for your machine)

1½-inch-wide (3.8 cm) metal brayer (roller)

Needle-nose pliers

Mallet

Fine-tip black marker

⅛-inch (3 mm) round hole drive punch

INSTRUCTIONS

1. Create a rectangular-shaped base by securing the two 1 x 8 x 16-inch (2.5 x 20.3 x 40.6 cm) pine boards upright between the 1 x 8 x 24-inch (2.5 x 20.3 x 61 cm) pine boards with the #8 wood screws and the handheld drill. Screw one of the ¾ x 18 x 24-inch (1.9 x 45.7 x 61 cm) pieces of plywood to the top.

2. Create a railing around the lip of the box by screwing on the two 1½ x 1½ x 15¼-inch (3.8 x 3.8 x 38.7 cm) rails to the shorter sides and the two 1½ x 1½ x 21¼-inch (3.8 x 3.8 x 54 cm) rails to the longer sides with the #8 wood screws.

3. Use rubber cement to glue the 18 x 24-inch (45.7 x 61 cm) foam pad to the remaining plywood board.

4. Spread out the quilt batting, and place the foam pad facedown in the center of it. Pull up the batting on opposite sides of the foam, and staple it in place on the board backing. Cut away the excess batting with fabric scissors, leaving about a 1-inch (2.5 cm) margin of batting. Pull up the batting on the remaining sides, and continue around all edges until the batting is tightly fitted.

5. Place the cowhide grain side down on the work surface. Center the cushion facedown on it, making sure that there is ample leather to pull up over the sides and onto the board backing.

6. Pull the leather up over opposite sides in the center, and staple it in place. Repeat this process on the other two sides, leaving the corners unstapled. Gather the leather carefully around

each corner, and staple it in place. Continue to gather and staple the remaining leather until the leather is pulled tight all the way around the cushion. Use the leather shears to cut away the excess leather.

7. From the remaining cowhide, cut out two pieces of leather that measure 12 x 19 inches (30.5 x 48.3 cm) and two that measure 12 x 25 inches (30.5 x 63.5 cm).

8. Trim the width of several sticky notes to 4 inches (10.2 cm). Place the notes along the length of each of the leather pieces as follows: on each 12 x 19-inch (30.5 x 48.3 cm) piece, center the notes, placing them 2 inches (5.1 cm) from each end and 1½ inches (3.8 cm) apart; on each 12 x 25-inch (30.5 x 63.5 cm) piece, center the notes, placing them 1½ inches (3.8 cm) from the ends and 1¹⁄₁₆ inches (2.7 cm) apart. Make certain that the top edges of the notes are parallel to the top of the leather, since you'll use their placement to determine where you apply your stamps.

9. Squeeze out a dollop of black fabric paint onto a slick surface such as a piece of glass or an old ceramic plate. Rock the rubber brayer back and forth in the paint to spread it evenly. Use it to apply a thin, even coat of paint to the surface of the stamp (photo 1).

10. Remove one of the sticky notes and stamp the image in its place, being careful to align the image with the edges of the leather. Repeat this process to add the repeated design across each of the leather sections. Allow the stamped surface to dry.

11. Use the fine-tip "liner" paintbrush to add metallic accents to the stamped images.

12. Place the right sides together of one of the short and one of the long pieces of leather that you cut in step 7. Use the sewing machine equipped with a leather needle to sew together the 12-inch (30.5 cm) ends of the pieces with a ½-inch (1.3 cm) seam. Tie off the threads at the end of each seam (photo 2). Repeat this process to sew together the other two short and long pieces. Then sew the two assembled leather pieces together at the remaining edges to form a circular piece.

13. Apply rubber cement underneath the seams, and press them down with your fingers (photo 3). Roll out the seams with the metal brayer (photo 4). On the front of the leather piece at the four seams, use the sewing machine to sew two lines of topstitching ⅛-inch (3 mm) on either side of the seam.

14. Cut two 12 x 40-inch (30.5 x 101.6 cm) pieces of batting. Wrap one of the batting pieces lengthwise around the sides of the rectangular base that you built in steps 1 and 2. Staple the batting to the top covered part of the base. Flip the base over and neatly wrap the batting over the edges, and staple it inside the open end of the base, 1 inch (2.5 cm) from the edge. Cut away the excess batting with scissors, leaving about a 1-inch (2.5 cm) margin.

15. Slip the stamped leather base cover around the sides of the rectangular wooden base. Pull up and staple the edge of the leather cover to the top of the base (photo 5). Flip the base over.

1

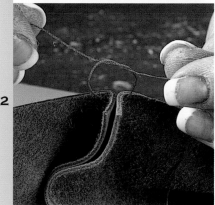

2

3

4

5

Staple the leather over the batting. Keep the edges and corners as smooth as possible, gathering the leather gradually in order to avoid areas of bulk. Use the leather shears to cut away the excess leather.

16. Around the leather-covered base, use the pliers and mallet to tap a brass upholstery tack into the center of each stamped image.

17. Place the cushion upside down with the base upside down on top of it. Use the handheld drill to insert the rough-thread deck screws inside the base at even intervals close to the walls to secure the cushion.

18. To cover the bottom of the base, fold the edges of the black upholstery fabric 1 inch (2.5 cm) around all sides, and secure it with staples.

19. Position the four top plates 1 inch (2.5 cm) from the outside edges of the corners. Mark the screw holes with the black marker. Where marked, use a ⅛-inch (3 mm) round hole drive punch and mallet to remove the leather and batting, exposing the wood. Predrill the holes with the handheld drill. Use the screwdriver to attach the top plates with the screws provided (see photo 6).

20. Screw each foot onto a top plate, slitting the black fabric to accommodate the feet as needed.

6

STAMPED RAWHIDE
CANDLE WRAP

THE PARCHMENT-LIKE EFFECT OF RAWHIDE IS

ENHANCED BY CANDLELIGHT. THIS SIMPLE LACING

PROJECT GIVES YOU ELEGANT RESULTS.

MATERIALS

Round candle votive, 4 x 4 inches (10.2 x 10.2 cm)

Piece of poster board

1 ounce (.41 mm) goat rawhide

1/8-inch (3 mm) rawhide lace, 20-inch (50.8 cm) piece

2 two-prong needles

Rubber stamp of your choice

White acylic paint

Cosmetic sponge

TOOLS AND SUPPLIES

Cloth tape measure

Pencil

Straightedge/ruler

Punch board

Craft or "clicker" knife

1/8-inch (3 mm) drive punch

Mallet

INSTRUCTIONS

1. Wrap the tape measure around the votive to determine its circumference. Add 1¼ inches (3.2 cm) to this measurement. (This will allow the ends of the rawhide panel to overlap when wrapped around the container.)

2. Use a pencil and straightedge to draw a rectangular shape on the poster board that is as high as the container and as wide as the measurement you determined in step 1.

3. Mark a vertical guideline next to one of the short edges that is ¼ inch (6 mm) from the edge. Draw another guideline ½ inch (1.3 cm) from the first one. On the opposite edge, mark one vertical guideline ⅜ inch (9.5 mm) from the edge. Draw another guideline ½-inch (1.3 cm) away from it.

4. Along all four guidelines, mark eight equally-spaced vertical holes on top of the punch board. Use the drive punch and mallet to punch out the holes.

5. Soak the rawhide in a clean tub of water until it becomes pliable. Transfer it to a large, clean cutting surface. Use the pattern as a guide to cut out the rawhide wrap with the knife and straightedge. Punch holes as designated on the pattern using the ⅛-inch (3 mm) drive punch.

6. Soak the rawhide lace in water for approximately 10 minutes or until it is pliable. Thread each of the lace ends onto a two-prong needle.

7. Wrap the rawhide around the container with the ⅜-inch (9.5 mm) edge overlapping the opposite edge.

8. Thread the lace from the underside of the wrap through the bottom two holes of both layers of rawhide, and pull the lace out so that it is centered.

9. Thread both lace ends in a criss-cross pattern (photo 1) until reaching the top edge of the rawhide. Secure the ends of lace with a knot (photo 2). (You can tie the knot on the outside of the wrap, or hide it inside.)

10. Once the rawhide has dried, apply white paint to the rubber stamp with a cosmetic sponge (photo 3). Stamp a decoative repeated image on the rawhide surface.

RAWHIDE
COVERED VASE

FOR A VARIATION OF THE RAWHIDE
CANDLE SHADE ON PAGE 104, LACE
UP A VASE WITH RAWHIDE AND USE
CONTRASTING LATIGO LACE FOR A
DIFFERENT LOOK. ADD EMBELLISH-
MENTS SUCH AS BUTTONS, LACE,
AND FEATHERS.

WOVEN SEAT STOOLS

COLORFUL PAINTED STRIPS OF LEATHER
MAKE A JAZZY EDITION TO A PLAIN BAR
STOOL. THIS IS A SIMPLE PROJECT THAT
YOU CAN DO WITHOUT A LOT OF FUSS.

MATERIALS

12 x 15-inch (30.5 x 38.1 cm) wooden stool with open seat (available at unfinished furniture stores)

Paint or varnish for finishing stool (if using unfinished wooden stool)

6 square feet (.54 m²) of 8- to 9-ounce (3.18 to 3.58 mm) vegetable-tanned leather

Fabric paint medium

Acrylic paint: yellow, turquoise, and purple

Spray acrylic leather finish

TOOLS AND SUPPLIES

Long straightedge/ruler

Craft or "clicker" knife

Paper or plastic sheets to cover work surface

4 empty containers (such as empty plastic tubs or yogurt containers)

Rubber gloves

Several foam-tip brushes

#1 edge beveler

Circle edge slicker

Staple gun

Staples

INSTRUCTIONS

1. If your stool is made of unfinished wood, paint or varnish it first. Allow the finish to dry thoroughly.

2. Use the straightedge and knife to cut out one 10 x 27-inch (25.4 x 68.6 cm) section and two 7 x 24-inch (17.8 x 61 cm) sections from the vegetable-tanned leather. (You'll be cutting strips from these sections later.)

3. Cover your work surface with paper or plastic sheets. Position the leather, grain or right side up, on your work surface.

4. Mix fabric paint medium with water following the manufacturer's instructions on the bottle, and place the mixture in one of the empty containers. In separate containers, mix each acrylic paint color with three parts of diluted fabric paint medium.

5. Put on rubber gloves. Choose one of the acrylic paint colors as the dominant one in the design of the stool. Use a foam-tip brush to apply the color to the 10 x 27-inch (25.4 x 68.6 cm) section of leather in a lengthwise direction. Set aside to dry. Apply each of the two remaining colors to the 7 x 24-inch (17.8 x 61 cm) sections of leather. Allow the leather to dry completely.

6. Cut six strips that measure 1⅜ x 26 inches (3.5 x 66 cm) from the larger 10 x 27-inch (25.4 x 68.6 cm) leather section (photo 1). Cut four strips of leather that measure 1⅜ x 23 inches (3.5 x 58.4 cm) from each 7 x 24-inch (17.8 x 61 cm) section of painted leather.

7. Use the #1 edge beveler to bevel the long edges of the strips (photo 1), and apply matching diluted paint to the edges with a foam-tip brush. Rub the circle edge slicker along the still-damp edges (photo 2). Allow the leather strips to dry completely.

8. Spray the surface of the leather strips with two light coats of acrylic finish.

9. Arrange the six longer strips on your work surface, colored side down, leaving about ⅛ inch (3 mm) between each strip. Flip the stool over, and place the shorter outside edges on the strips (photo 3).

10. Pull up one of the end strips that are adjacent to a corner post of the stool. Leave 1/16 inch (1.6 mm) between it and the edge of the corner post. Staple about 2 inches (5.1 cm) of the strip to the inside face of the frame to secure it. Continue to secure the strips along one edge, leaving ⅛ inch (3 mm) between each.

11. Flip the seat over, and repeat step 11 to secure the opposite end of each strip to the other side of the frame, pulling each length taut before stapling it. Remove the stool from your work surface.

12. Line up the two remaining colors of strips in a sequence of your choice, colored side down, leaving about ⅛ inch (3 mm) between each strip. Weave the strips between the ones that are in place (photo 4). Staple one end of the strip to the inside edge of the frame as described in step 11.

13. Once all of the strips have been woven, pull the end of each strip taut and staple it to the inside edge of the frame (photo 5). Continue this step with each woven strip until each has been secured.

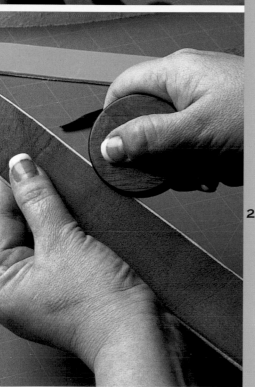

RAWHIDE PHOTO TRANSFER SCREEN

WHETHER YOU WANT TO CAPTURE YOUR DREAM OF BEING A COWGIRL OR SIMPLY SHOW OFF FAMILY PHOTOS, YOUR VERSION OF THIS SCREEN WILL BE AN UNDISPUTED CONVERSATION PIECE. IT COMBINES THE RAWHIDE LOOK OF AMERICAN'S WEST WITH THE CONTEMPORARY TECHNOLOGY OF PHOTO TRANSFER.

MATERIALS

3 salvage windows or doors with panes of glass removed (windows shown measure $5\frac{1}{2}$ feet high x $1\frac{1}{2}$ feet wide [1.7 x .4 m])

Spray satin varnish

Several pieces of poster board

$\frac{3}{32}$ x $\frac{1}{2}$-inch (2.4 mm x 1.3 cm) screw eyes

4 to 6 ounces (112 to 168 g) cream-colored rawhide

$\frac{5}{16}$-inch (8 mm) brass grommets (You must calculate the number needed for your particular piece after making the panel patterns described in step 2 of the directions.)

$\frac{1}{8}$-inch (3 mm) red latigo lace (You must calculate the amount needed as described in step 8 in the directions.)

Photos and fabric of your choice for image transfer

12 x 18-inch (30.5 x 45.7 cm) transfer paper made for artists (available at fine art supply stores)

Turpentine

6 screen/piano hinges with screws

TOOLS AND SUPPLIES

Measuring tape

Pencil

Straightedge/ruler

Craft knife or "clicker" knife

Small handheld drill

Pliers

Large plastic tub

Tools and Supplies continued on the next page

Several old towels

Punch board

¼-inch (6 mm) round drive punch

Mallet

Grommet setter made for setting ⁵⁄₁₆-inch (8 mm) grommets

Leather shears

Foam paint roller

Newsprint paper

2-inch (5.1 cm) paintbrush

Screwdriver

INSTRUCTIONS

1. Wash the surfaces of your doors or windows thoroughly to remove any dirt or flaking paint. Once dry, seal the surfaces with satin varnish.

2. Measure the inside dimensions of each window opening, and subtract 2 inches (5.1 cm) from the width and length. With the straightedge and a pencil, draw patterns on the poster board using the measurements. (If all the openings are the same, as they are on our piece, then you'll only need one pattern.) Cut the patterns out.

3. On the pattern(s), make marks around the edges that are spaced 2 inches (5.1 cm) apart and ½ inch (1.3 cm) from the edge. (These marks indicate where the grommets will go in the rawhide panels.)

4. Place the doors or windows flat on the floor, and position each of the patterns or the single pattern in the center of its opening. Inside the wooden frame, make pencil marks along the edges directly above or to the side of each of the pattern's grommet marks to indicate where the screw eyes will go. Use the handheld drill to predrill all of these holes inside the frame of each window. Screw in each screw eye, and tighten with pliers.

5. Fill the tub with clean water. Prepare the rawhide by soaking it until it becomes pliable. Transfer it to a large, clean cutting surface.

6. Use the poster board patterns, the straightedge, and a knife to cut out each rawhide panel. Dampen the towels, and place the panels between them to keep the waiting rawhide panels pliable as you work on each.

7. Place the punch board on your work surface. Use the ¼-inch (6 mm) round drive punch to punch holes in the rawhide where indicated on the pattern(s). Use the grommet setter and mallet to attach the grommets to each rawhide panel (photo 1).

8. Next, you'll lace the sides of each rawhide panel to the screweyes that you secured in each of the openings. Calculate how much lace to cut by multiplying the length of each inside edge (whether width or length) by three. Cut a corresponding piece of lace for each width or length.

9. Place the rawhide panels in each of their openings on the floor or your work surface. Thread one end of the matching lace lengths by hand through the front of a corner grommet, and tie off the end of the lace on the back to hold it in place. Push the long end of the lace through the corresponding grommet from the back and out the front. Then move diagonally to the next hole up, and push the lace through the front of the grommet. Go back through the corresponding screw eye from the back. Continue this process until you reach the last hole on the other side of the panel. Make certain that the panel is still centered, and then tie off the other end of the lace so that it is taut but not tight. Check to make sure that it is about 2 inches (5.1 cm) from the center of each grommet hole to the center of each screw eye (photo 2).

10. Repeat this lacing process on the opposite side, pulling the lace taut but not tight. Lace the remaining two

sides. Repeat this process to place the rawhide panels in all of the openings. After you've finished, allow the rawhide to dry completely.

11. Photocopy the selected images onto pieces of transfer paper. Cut out the images. Arrange them on the panels as you would like them to be in the final piece.

12. Soak each trimmed paper image in water for about a minute so that the film floats away from the paper. Use the foam roller to apply a light coat of turpentine to the surface of the rawhide where you plan to place the image.

13. Carefully remove the film from the water, and place it between newsprint paper to remove the excess water. Slide each image off of the paper and gently position it on the rawhide.

Warning: The film will quickly adhere to the rawhide surface, so you won't be able to reposition it once it is placed.

14. Use the paintbrush to apply a thin coat of turpentine to the image. Leave the screen flat until the rawhide is completely dry.

15. Use the handheld drill and screwdriver to attach the three finished screen panels at each of the two joining edges with one hinge about 3 inches (7.6 cm) from the top, one in the middle, and one about 3 inches (7.6 cm) from the bottom.

1

2

Wearable Art

Perforated Suede Wrap

Wrap yourself in this gorgeous silk and suede piece of wearable art that is finished with a striking border design accented with pearl and seed beads. It is the embodiment of elegance—from the way that it looks and feels to the way that it hangs.

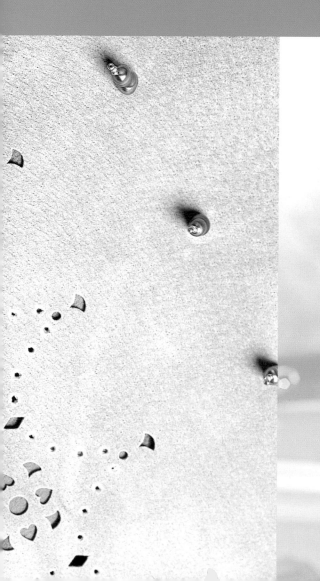

Materials

Repeating pattern (see page 134)

Piece of poster board

15 square feet (1.4 square meters) of pewter-colored pig suede

Polyester thread to match suede

2 yards (1.8 m) of teal-colored silk

Polyester thread to match silk

Neutral nylon beading thread

Pewter natural pearls

Pewter and teal seed beads (size 11)

Tools and Supplies

Glue stick

Punch board

Round hole drive punches in the following sizes: 1/16 inch (1.6 mm), 5/64 inch (2 mm), 1/8 inch (3 mm), 1/4 inch (6 mm)

Oblong punch, 1/2 inch (1.3 cm)

Decorative punches: heart-shaped, pie-shaped, and diamond-shaped

Mallet

Craft knife or leather shears

Sewing machine with needle suited for sewing silk as well as size 14 leather needle (or needle appropriate for your machine)

Medium binder clips

Fabric scissors

Straight pins

Clothes iron

Nylon thread

Sharp needle

Rubber cement

1½-inch-wide (3.8 cm) metal brayer (roller)

Cotton cloth or pillowcase

INSTRUCTIONS

1. Use the glue stick to adhere the pattern to the poster board. Place the punch board on your work surface and punch through each hole with the designated punch as indicated on the pattern. Use the knife to cut away the excess poster board, leaving a 1-inch (2.5 cm) margin around the perforated holes.

2. Use the craft knife or leather shears to cut one 21 x 40-inch (53.3 x 101.6 cm) and two 21 x 30-inch (53.3 x 76.2 cm) panels from the suede.

3. Lay out the larger piece of suede lengthwise between the two smaller pieces. Use the sewing machine equipped with leather needle to sew together the adjoining seams (right sides together) with a ½-inch-wide (1.3 cm) mock flat-fell seam (see page 22).

4. Position the suede on the punch board right side up (showing finished seams) with one of the 21-inch (53.3 cm) edges in a horizontal position on the board. Beginning at the left end of this side, place the perforated poster board pattern 1 inch (2.5 cm) from the bottom edge and 1½ inches (3.8 cm) from the left edge. Use the binder clips to hold the pattern in place.

5. Punch the perforated pattern with the designated punches. Reposition the pattern to the right of the holes so that it repeats the pattern in an uninterrupted fashion. Continue to punch the holes in a repeated pattern across the suede, leaving a 1½-inch (3.8 cm) margin on the right side (photo 1).

6. Use the pattern to punch an identical perforated pattern on the opposite side of the suede piece.

7. Use the fabric scissors to cut two 21 x 57-inch (53.3 x 144.8 cm) pieces from the teal-colored silk. Fit the machine with the needle for sewing silk, and thread it with teal thread. Place the right sides of two of the 21-inch-long (53.3 cm) sides together, and hold in place with straight pins. Sew together with a ½-inch-wide (1.3 cm) French seam (see page 22).

8. Heat the clothes iron to a setting that is appropriate for silk. Fold and press a 1-inch (2.5 cm) hem toward the wrong side on each 21-inch (53.3 cm) end of the silk piece. Fold and press a 6-inch-wide (15.2 cm) hem on the same ends. Use an appliqué needle and the teal thread to blind stitch the hem by hand.

9. Place the wrong sides of the suede and silk panels together, and use binder clips to hold them in place along the long edges. Use the sewing machine equipped with the leather needle to sew them together with a ½-inch (1.3 cm) seam. Tie square knots in the threads to secure them.

10. Press back the suede seam allowance with your fingers, and baste it in place with rubber cement and the brayer. Once the cement is dry, finger press the silk seam allowance back, then place a cloth or pillowcase over it to protect the silk while you press it out with the iron.

11. Turn the silk and suede right side out, and press the silk side seams again as needed.

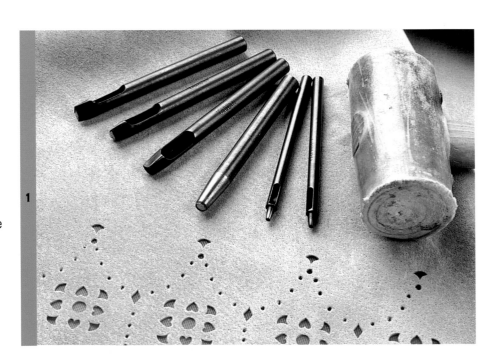

12. Thread a single strand of nylon thread onto the sharp needle. Reach inside the silk and suede tube, and thread the needle through the back side of the suede, 1½ inches (3.8 cm) from the crest of the perforated design (see pattern). Tie a knot in the thread, and pull it close to the suede.

13. Slide a natural pewter-colored pearl, a pewter seed bead, a teal seed bead, and another pewter seed beed on the nylon thread. Skip the last seed bead that you put on, and thread the needle back through the remaining three beads to the back of the suede. Leave the needle on the thread, and tie off the thread several times close to the suede.

14. Move across to the next position for beading, come up through the suede with the needle, and continue beading (photo 2). Finish this beading pattern on both ends of the wrap.

15. To hem the bottom edges with a decorated whipstitch, thread a sequence of three pewter, three teal, and three pewter beads between each stitch along the entire hem (photo 3). Repeat this step to finish the opposite edge (photo 4).

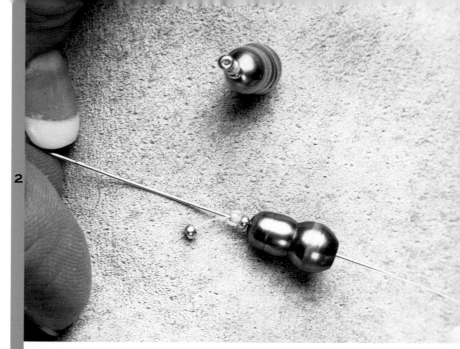

2

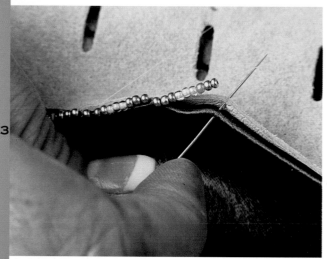

3

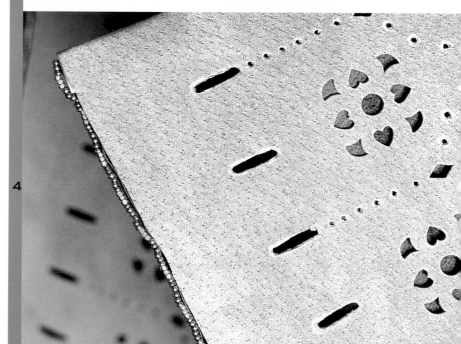

4

MATERIALS

Patterns (see pages 135 and 136)

Piece of poster board

2 square feet (.18 m²) of tan deer-tanned cowhide

1 square foot (.09 m²) of pig suede in each of the following colors: red, purple, black

Upholstery/nylon tan thread

2 metal hoops, 5-inch (12.7 cm) diameter

2 yards (1.8 m) of ⅛-inch (3 mm) latigo lace in tan

TOOLS AND SUPPLIES

Glue stick

Craft or "clicker" knife

Straightedge/ruler

Rubber cement

Stack of books or object to use as weight

Sewing machine fitted with size 16 leather needle (or needle appropriate for your machine)

Contact cement

1½-inch-wide (3.8 cm) metal brayer (roller)

Leather shears

⅛-inch (3 mm) drive punch

Mallet

Punch board

2 clothespins

Small binder clips

Threaded lacing needle

APPLIQUÉD HANDBAG

THIS SPLASHY LEATHER AND SUEDE PURSE IS SIMPLER TO MAKE THAN IT APPEARS TO BE. AND, IT WILL MAKE A DISTINCT IMPRESSION WHEREVER YOU ROAM.

INSTRUCTIONS

1. Glue the patterns for the handbag's front and back, the straps, and the appliqué shapes to the poster board, and cut them out with the knife and straightedge.

2. Use the patterns as a guide to cut out the front and back, the two center straps, and four curved side straps from the cowhide.

3. From the cowhide, cut two leather thongs that are 2 yards (1.8 m) long and ½ inch (1.3 cm) wide.

4. Following the colors indicated on the patterns, cut out the colored suede appliqué shapes.

5. Using the finished piece as a guide, use rubber cement to baste the suede shapes onto the handbag's front piece (photo 1). Place the books or other weight on the piece until it dries.

6. Appliqué each basted shape onto the front by machine stitching close to the edge of each shape in tan thread.

7. Apply an even coat of contact cement to the center portion of each of the six straps. Once the cement becomes tacky, fold in a quarter of the width of each strap toward the center, aligning the edges in the middle (photo 2). Roll out the seams with the metal brayer (photo 3). Repeat this step for each of the five remaining straps. Place the straps under a weight until they are dry.

8. Use leather shears to trim the ends of the straps to obtain a straight, blunt edge.

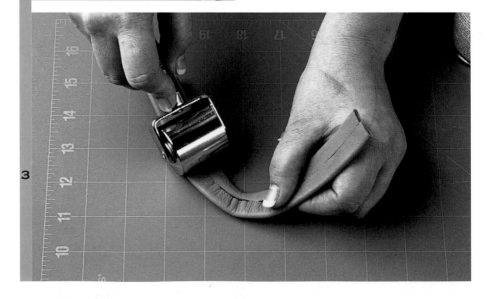

9. Use the patterns as a guide to punch four holes at the end of the six straps with a ⅛-inch (3 mm) drive punch.

10. To wrap each of the metal rings with one of the 2-yard (1.8 m) lengths of leather thong, apply a light coat of contact cement to the back of each thong. Wrap and secure the end of each thong to a metal ring, holding it in place with a clothespin (photo 4). Wrap the remainder of each thong, overlapping it slightly as you go.

11. On the appliquéd front and the plain back of the handbag pieces, apply an even coat of contact cement on the back of each flap's top edge. Fold each flap down, and press it into place. Use a ⅛-inch (3 mm) drive punch to punch three sets of four holes through the top of the front and the back as marked on the pattern.

12. Place the right sides of the front and back together, and hold the side and bottom edges together with binder clips.

13. Use the sewing machine and tan thread to stitch around the three edges of the handbag with a ½-inch (1.3 cm) seam allowance.

14. Use the leather shears to cut six 12-inch (30.5 cm) lengths from the latigo lace. Attach the threaded lacing needle to one of the lace lengths.

15. Loop one of the center straps over one of the covered rings. Position one end of the strap on the front of the bag, aligning it with the punched holes. Position the other end of the strap on the backside of the front, aligning it with the punched holes.

16. Pull the lace through one of the top holes in the strap from the backside of the bag, leaving a tail of about 4 inches (10.2 cm). Crisscross over to the hole that is diagonal to the top

hole, push the thread through, and then come back to the front through the adjacent hole. Crisscross to the remaining top hole, and push the thread through to the back. Remove the needle, and tie an overhand knot in the lace to secure the strap. Use leather shears to trim the lace ends (photo 5).

17. Repeat steps 15 and 16 to add the center strap and ring to the back of the bag. Then add the remaining curved straps in the same way, making sure that they curve in toward the center strap (photo 6).

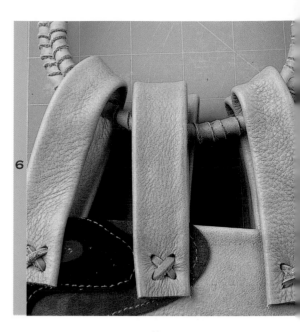

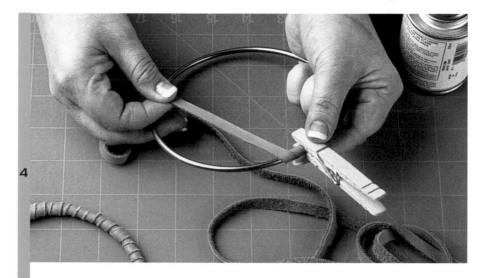

STENCILED HANDBAG

USE CONTEMPORARY STENCILING AND A TRADITIONAL SADDLE STITCH TO MAKE THIS BEAUTIFUL BEADED BAG.

MATERIALS

Patterns (see page 137)

Piece of poster board

Black leather solvent-based "spirit" dye

2 square feet (1.8m²) of 2- to 3-ounce (.78 to 1.19mm) vegetable-tanned leather

Stencil with design of your choice

1 square foot (.9 m²) dark tan garment suede

Stencil paint: black, metallic gold

Leather wax

Black waxed thread

Two 30-inch-long (76.2 cm) pieces of nylon-coated beading wire

40 black opaque beads (6 mm)

4 crimp beads

82 black beads with gold center stripe (11 mm)

4 large black glass beads

TOOLS AND SUPPLIES

Glue stick	Soft rag
Craft or "clicker" knife	2 large eye sewing needles
Straight edge/ruler	Scratch awl
Wool scraps	Contact cement
Punch board	Stitching pony
¹⁄₁₆-inch (1.6 mm) drive punch	Needle-nose pliers
Mallet	
2 round stencil brushes	
Foam-tip brush	

INSTRUCTIONS

1. Glue the patterns for the handbag to the poster board, and cut them out with the knife and straightedge.

2. Use the wool to apply two coats of black leather dye to a portion of the front of the vegetable-tanned leather that is large enough for cutting out two borders for the bag from the pattern provided. Allow the leather dry completely between coats. Use the pattern, knife, and straightedge to cut out two black border pieces.

3. Use the pattern to cut out the two center pieces from the garment suede.

4. Place the punch board on your work surface. Punch the 1/16-inch (1.6 mm) holes indicated on the pattern around the center suede pieces with the punch and mallet (photo 1). Repeat this process to punch the holes indicated on the pattern around both edges of the black border pieces.

5. Position the stencil on the front of one of the dark tan suede pieces.

6. Use one of the stencil brushes and black stencil paint to pounce on a light application in the open areas of the stencil, leaving small areas blank to fill in with gold (photo 2). Use the other stencil brush to apply metallic gold stencil paint as a highlight to the areas that you left blank (photo 3).

7. Reposition the stencil, and apply stencil paint until you are satisfied with the depth of the design. Allow the paint to completely dry. (If heat setting is required by the paint manufacturer, do it once you've finished.)

8. Use a foam-tip brush and some of the black leather dye to touch up the cut edges around the black border pieces, and allow it to dry.

9. To seal and protect the surface, apply an even coat of leather wax with a soft rag to the dyed surface and buff.

10. Cut off a 78-inch (198.1 cm) length of black waxed thread. Thread both ends of the length with a large needle.

11. Position one of the black border pieces on top of each of the stencilled suede pieces, aligning the punched holes. Apply contact cement underneath the edges of the black pieces, and press them into place.

12. Position and clamp one of the sides of the handbag in the stitching pony upside down with the stencilled side facing the hand that you use to write with.

13. First you'll saddle stitch the center suede panels to the black borders. To begin stitching, hold both needles on the back, unstencilled side of the panel. Use the awl as needed to enlarge the holes as needed. Thread one needle through a hole along the bottom inside edge of the handbag from the back, pulling the thread halfway through. Thread the same needle through the next hole, and pull the lace halfway through so that a loop hangs out the back side. Thread the needle coming out of the first hole in the second hole, and pull both thread lengths snug.

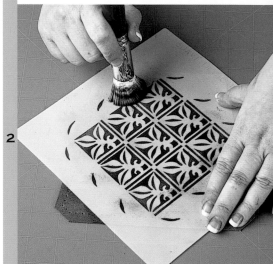

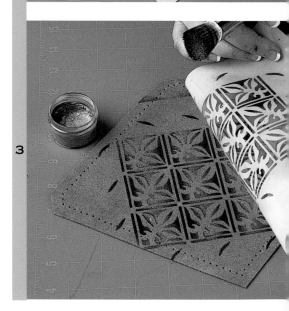

14. Continue to thread each needle from opposite directions through each hole and pull snug to continue saddle stitching around the bag's frame. Reposition and secure the bag in the stitching pony as needed.

15. To end and tie off the saddle stitch, backstitch through the last two holes. Pull both of the thread ends tight, and cut the thread flush to the leather surface.

16. Repeat steps 13 through 15 for the second panel.

17. Once the bag's front and back panels have been stitched, fold down and align the holes of the tabs for the handles. Secure them with contact cement.

18. Use contact cement to baste the bottom edge and sides of the handbag together.

19. Clamp the two sides of the handbag into the stitching pony with right sides out and the top of the bag up, aligning the edges. Cut off a 96-inch (243.8 cm) length of thread. Thread a large needle onto both ends of the thread length as you did in step 10.

20. Begin the next process by saddle stitching one of the top edges (the edges that will be open, not sewn together). Pull one of the needles through both layers of leather at one of the top corners (photo 4). Then stitch one of the top edges (photo 5).

21. Upon reaching the second to last hole on the opposite corner, stitch through the two layers of leather as you did in step 20.

22. Continue to saddle stitch around the corner of the handbag through two layers to connect the side, bottom, and other side of the handbag. When you reach the corner hole along the top edge, make two stitches through both layers of leather then resume saddle stitching through the single layer of leather on the unstitched side of the top edge. End the stitching with two back stitches. Cut off the excess thread close to the leather surface.

23. Cut two 30-inch (76.2 cm) lengths of beading wire. Thread ten of the 6 mm black beads and a crimp bead onto one of the ends of each of the wires. Thread each end of the beaded wire through one of the leather loops on opposite sides along the top edge of the handbag.

24. To make a circular loop out of the beads, thread 2 inches (5 cm) of the wire end back through each of the crimp beads, pulling the slack from beaded wire. Use the needle-nose pliers to flatten each of the crimp beads and secure the wire (photo 6).

25. On each of the wires, thread on one large black glass bead followed by half of the black and gold beads. End with another large glass bead. Add ten more 6 mm black beads and a crimp bead through the leather loops to finish off the end of each handle the way that you began it.

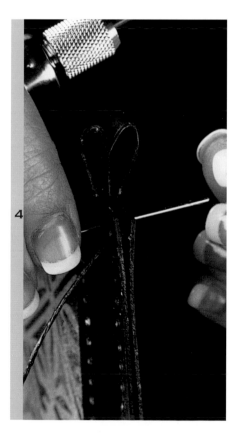

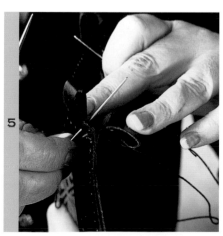

PERFORATED DRAWSTRING POUCH

THIS SOFT POUCH OF GOLD AND BLACK SPORTS A SNAPPY PUNCHED DESIGN ON ALL FOUR SIDES THAT IS SILHOUETTED BY ITS BLACK SUEDE LINING. STRAPS WEIGHTED WITH BLACK BEADS AND TASSELS ARE BOTH FUNCTIONAL AND SASSY.

MATERIALS

Patterns (see pages 138 and 139)

Piece of poster board

3 square feet (.27 m²) each of kidskin in gold and black

$5/16$-inch (8 mm) brass grommets

2 yards (1.8 m) of $3/16$-inch (4.8 mm) cable cord

Clear nylon thread

4 large black beads

2-inch-wide (5.1 cm) black leather fringe, 16-inch-long (40.6 m) piece

TOOLS AND SUPPLIES

Glue stick

Craft or "clicker" knife

Straightedge/ruler

Punch board

Round drive punches in the following sizes: $1/16$ inch (1.6 mm), $3/32$ inch (2.4 mm), $1/8$ inch (3 mm), $5/32$ inch (4 mm), $1/4$ inch (6 mm), and $5/16$ inch (8 mm)

$3/8$-inch (9.5 mm) decorative punches: teardrop, moon, pie

Mallet

Rubber cement

Grommet setter made for $5/16$-inch (8 mm) grommets

Binder clips

Threaded lacing needle

Leather shears

Contact cement

Glover's needle

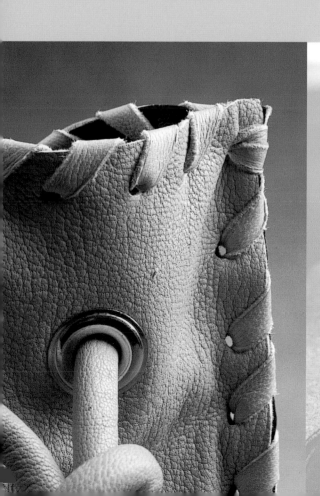

1. Make sure that your enlarged patterns measure 6½ inches (16.5 cm) square for the base pieces and 6 x 10 inches (15.2 x 25.4 cm) for the side panels. Glue each pattern to the poster board, and cut it out with the knife and straightedge.

2. Use the designated punches to punch the holes in the side panel and base patterns as indicated: ⁵⁄₃₂-inch (4 mm) holes at the corners and ⅛-inch (3 mm) holes along the edges. Punch the perforated pattern in the side panel pattern using the decorative punches as shown.

3. Use the base pattern and knife to cut out a square from the gold kidskin and a square from the black kidskin. Use the side panel pattern to cut out four panels from the gold kidskin and four from the black kidskin.

4. Place the punch board on your work surface. Using the pattern as a guide, use the ⁵⁄₃₂-inch (4 mm) punch to make the holes in the corners of all ten pieces of leather (eight gold side panels, eight black side panels, one gold base panel, and one black base panel). Use the ⅛-inch (3 mm) drive punch to make the holes that lie ¼ inch (6 mm) from all the edges and ½ inch (1.3 cm) apart.

5. Punch out the grommet holes where indicated on the pattern with the ¼-inch (6 mm) punch on all eight of the rectangular panels.

6. Position the rectangular pattern on one of the gold rectangular pieces, and punch out the decorative pattern with the punches specified on the pattern. (See photo 1 that shows one perforated gold piece and accompanying black piece, two pieces for the bottom of the pouch with punched holes, and punches with pattern ready to perforate second gold panel). Punch the remaining gold panel.

7. With the wrong sides together, place each of the gold perforated panels onto a black rectangular panel. Align the holes, and use rubber cement to baste together the edges of the four double-thickness panels.

8. Use the grommet setter to set the brass grommets in the holes that you punched in step 4.

9. Place the square base with the black side up on your work surface. With the grommets at the top, place the bottom of the bag onto the square base with the black interior sides facing one another. Baste the edges in place with rubber cement, and clip with binder clips until the cement dries.

10. From the gold kidskin, use the knife to cut out two 2-yard (1.8 m) lengths and four 1-yard (.9 m) lengths of ½-inch (1.3 cm) thong for lacing (photo 2). The shorter lengths will be used for lacing the sides, and the longer lengths will be used for lacing the top and base of the pouch.

11. Attach a threaded lacing needle onto the end of one of the shorter lengths of thong. Knot the end of the thong.

12. Reach inside the pouch, and thread the needle out through one of the corner holes of one of the side panels, leaving a 2-inch (5.1 cm) lace end

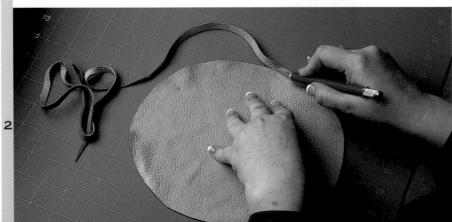

on the inside of the bag. Thread the needle into the adjacent corner hole on the next panel. Pull the thong snug. Thread the needle over the lace end and back out through the first corner hole, pulling the end of the thong tight and securing the lace end.

13. Following the lines of perforated holes, whipstitch up the side of the pouch. Finish off the end of the thong by doubling through the corner holes as you did at the beginning of the line of stitching. Tie a knot in the thong on the inside, and trim the end close to the knot with the leather shears.

14. Repeat steps 11 through 13 to lace up the remaining three sides of the pouch.

15. To lace the base to the sides, thread the needle with lace and pull through a center hole at the bottom of one of the side panels. Leave a 2-inch (5.1 cm) length of lace inside the bag. Position the end of the lace so that it will be secured underneath the lace as you whipstitch around the base of the pouch. When you reach the starting point of the lace, thread the needle through the last and first hole twice. Secure the lace end inside the bag under the stitches. Trim away the excess lace with leather shears.

16. Attach a new lace to the needle to lace the top edge. Thread the needle from inside the pouch in the center of one of the side panels at the top. Secure the end of the thread under the stitches as you whipstitch around the edge. When you reach the starting point of the stitching, secure the lace end as you did in step 12.

17. Cut two 1 x 30-inch (2.5 x 76.2 cm) strips of gold kidskin. (If your kidskin cannot provide a 30-inch (76.2 cm) length, or you want to make a longer drawstring, cut two strips that can be overlapped and cemented together.)

18. Cut two 30-inch (76.2 cm) lengths of cable cord. Place one of the 30-inch (76.2 cm) long kidskin strips facedown on the work surface, and apply an even coat of contact cement along the length of it. Position one of the cords along the edge. Tightly roll the kidskin strip around the cord, adding more contact cement as needed to hold the leather in place. Once the kidskin is secured around the cord, roll and firmly press the cord forward on the surface with the palm of your hands. Allow the cord to dry completely. Repeat this process to cover the second cable cord with kidskin (photo 3).

19. Unwrap 2½ inches (6.4 cm) of each end of the wrapped cords. At an angle, cut through the cord only to remove a portion of it and thin it out. Taper each of the kidskin wraps to a point that is 1 inch (2.5 cm) longer than the cords.

20. Thread clear nylon thread on the glover's needle, and backstitch along the length of the edges of the leather cord, stopping short of the cut portion.

21. Beginning on any of the four side panels, thread one of the kidskin cords through the four grommets on one side of the pouch, coming out the other side of the pouch. Thread the remaining cord through the other side of the pouch (photo 4).

22. Twist the end of one of the cords to a point and attach the threaded lacing needle to the cord. Thread the needle through one of the large black beads, and remove the needle. Pull the pointed leather end as far as it will go through the bead. Add black beads to the other three cords.

23. Cut the black fringe into 4-inch-long (10.2 cm) pieces. Place the fringe facedown on your work surface, and apply contact cement to the length of the base of the fringe. Beginning at one end of the piece of fringe, tightly wrap it around the length of one of the kidskin cord ends that protrudes from a black bead. Allow the cement to dry. Repeat to add fringe to the other three cords. Use the leather shears to trim away the excess gold kidskin cord inside the black fringe.

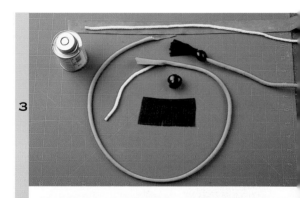

3

4

CURTAIN TIEBACKS WITH PAINTED DESIGNS (PAGE 34)

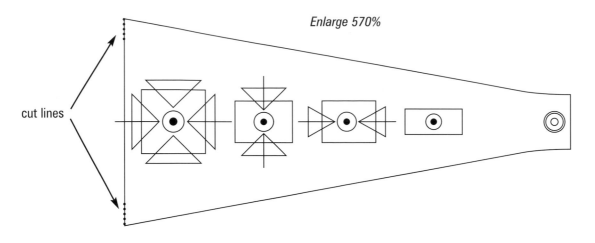

Enlarge 570%

cut lines

PAINTED TABLE RUNNER (PAGE 36)

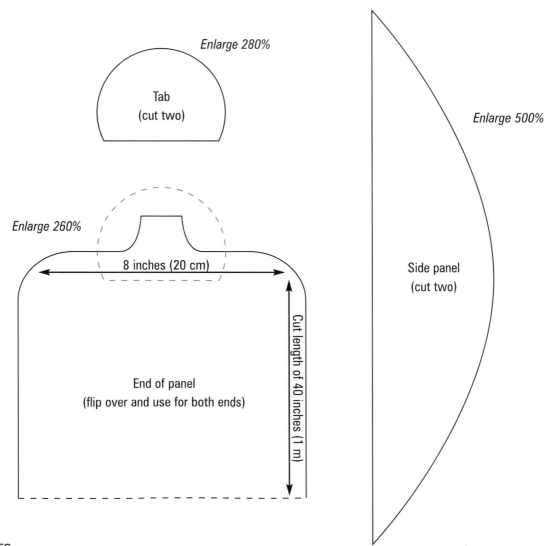

Enlarge 280%

Tab
(cut two)

Enlarge 260%

Enlarge 500%

Side panel
(cut two)

8 inches (20 cm)

End of panel
(flip over and use for both ends)

Cut length of 40 inches (1 m)

Templates

SCONCE OR CHANDELIER SHADES (PAGE 40)

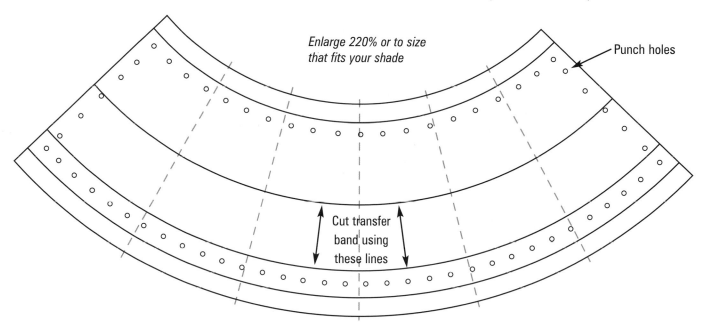

*Enlarge 220% or to size
that fits your shade*

Punch holes

Cut transfer
band using
these lines

BRANDED AND PAINTED PLACE MATS (PAGE 46)

Enlarge 400%

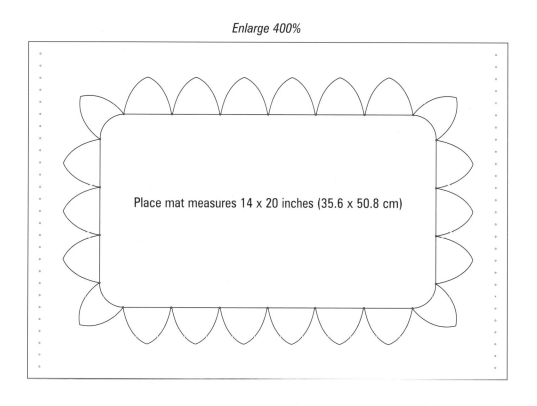

Place mat measures 14 x 20 inches (35.6 x 50.8 cm)

BRANDED AND PAINTED NAPKIN CUFFS (PAGE 50)

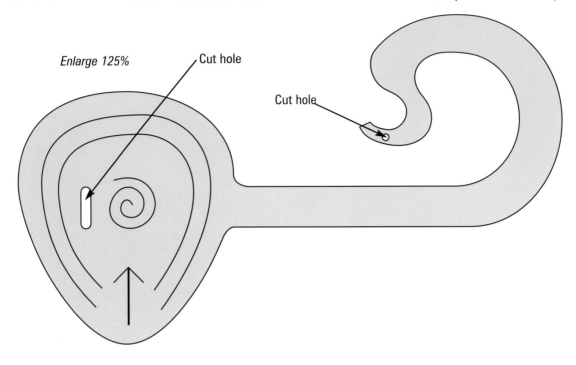

Enlarge 125%

Cut hole

Cut hole

TOOLED FRAME (PAGE 64)

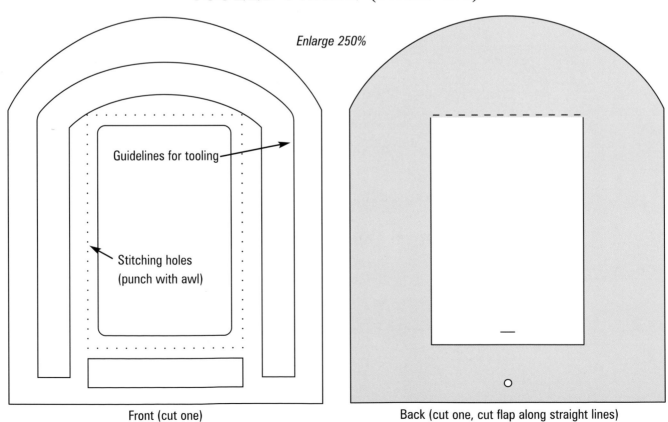

Enlarge 250%

Guidelines for tooling

Stitching holes
(punch with awl)

Front (cut one)

Back (cut one, cut flap along straight lines)

Appliquéd Suede Throw (page 84)

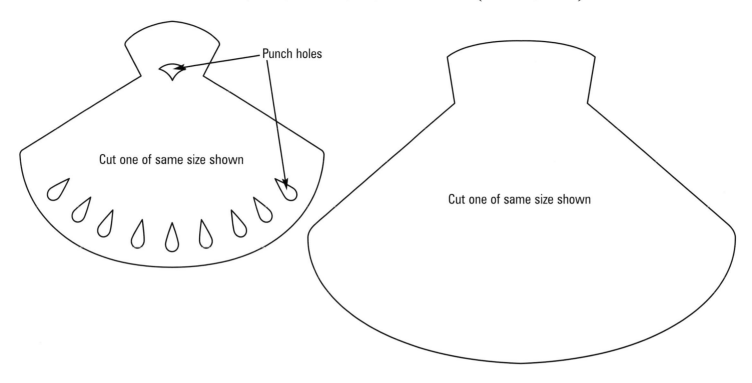

Punch holes

Cut one of same size shown

Cut one of same size shown

Stenciled Frame with Mirror (page 88)

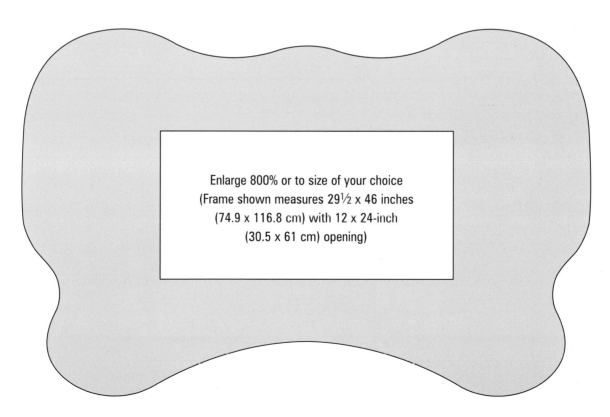

Enlarge 800% or to size of your choice
(Frame shown measures 29½ x 46 inches
(74.9 x 116.8 cm) with 12 x 24-inch
(30.5 x 61 cm) opening)

PHOTO TRANSFER PILLOWS (PAGE 92)

Enlarge 340%

Pillow front
(cut one for each pillow)

PERFORATED SUEDE WRAP (PAGE 114)

Enlarge 150%

Edge of wrap (punch holes as indicated on both ends of suede)

Enlarge 200%

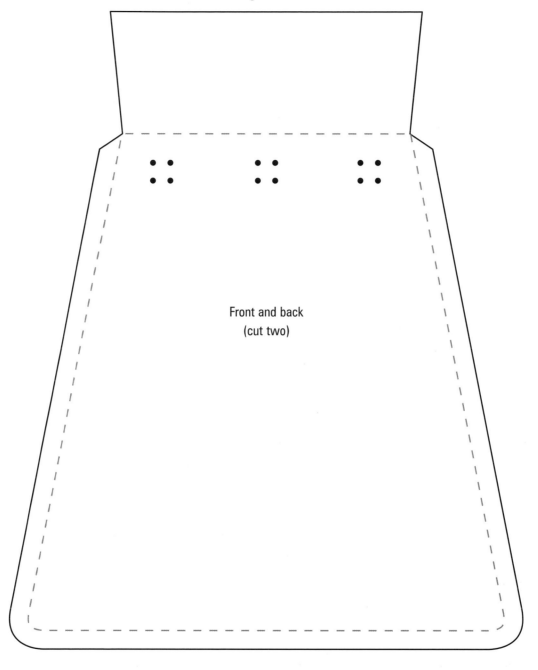

Front and back
(cut two)

APPLIQUÉD HANDBAG (PAGE 118)

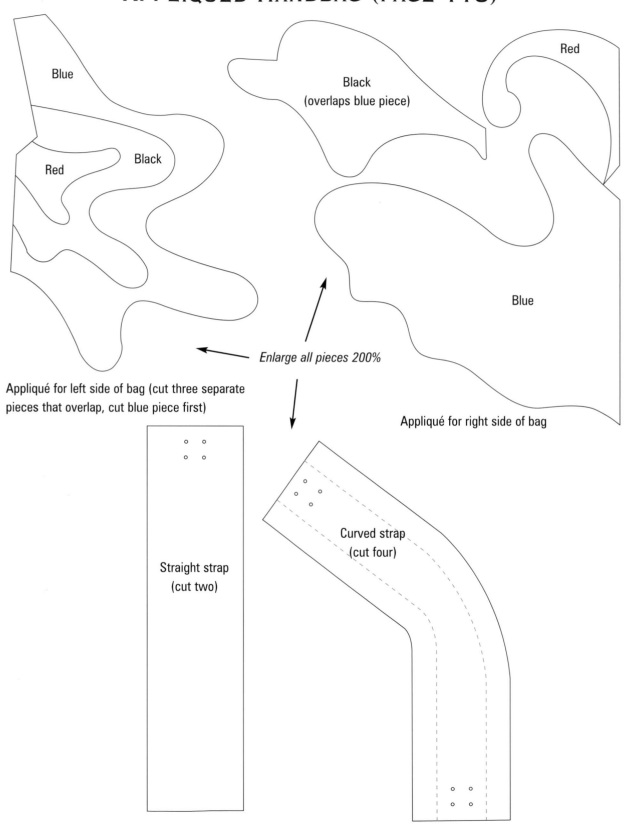

Blue

Red

Black

Black
(overlaps blue piece)

Red

Blue

Enlarge all pieces 200%

Appliqué for left side of bag (cut three separate
pieces that overlap, cut blue piece first)

Appliqué for right side of bag

Straight strap
(cut two)

Curved strap
(cut four)

Stenciled Handbag (page 122)

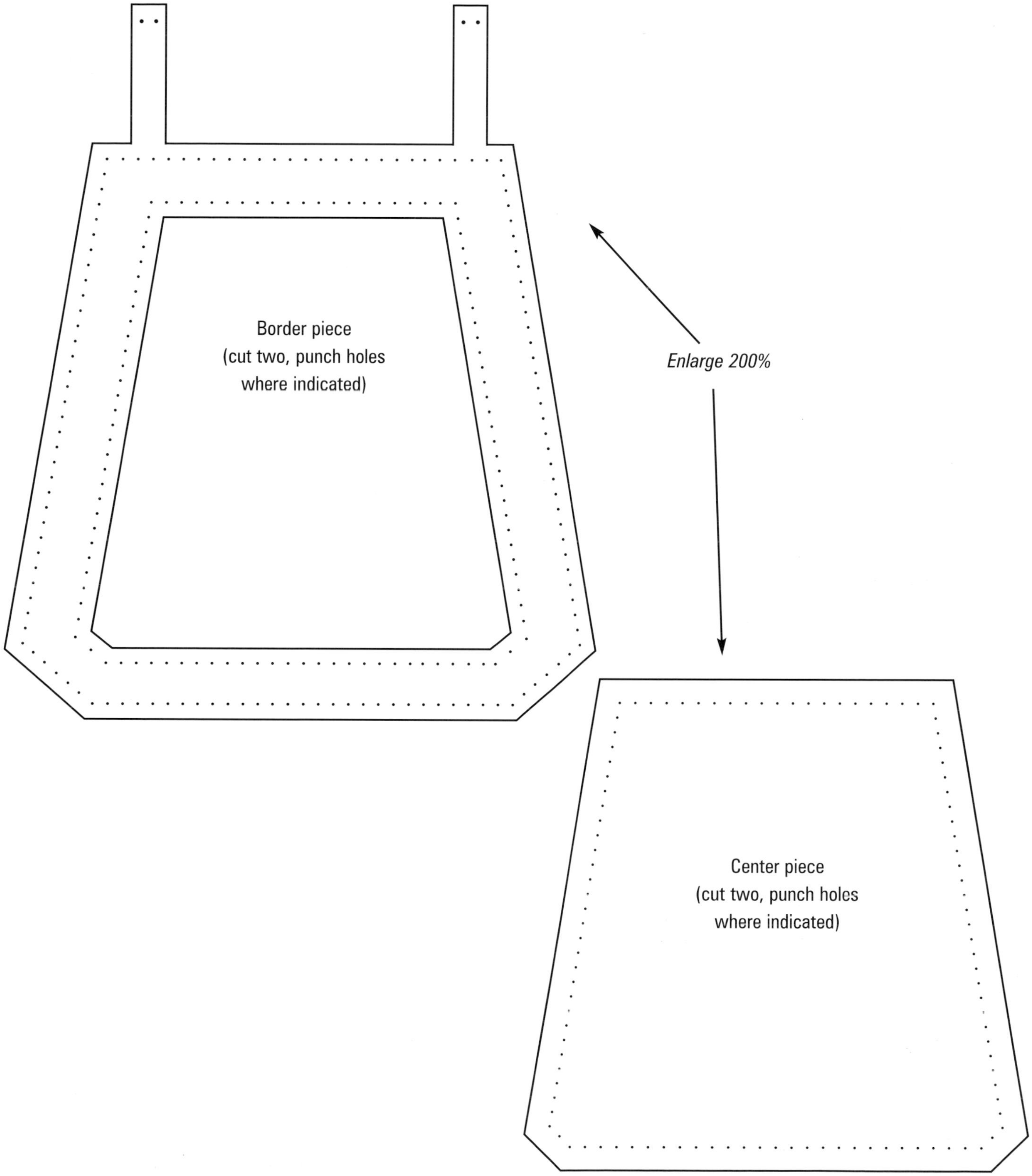

Border piece
(cut two, punch holes
where indicated)

Enlarge 200%

Center piece
(cut two, punch holes
where indicated)

Enlarge 125%

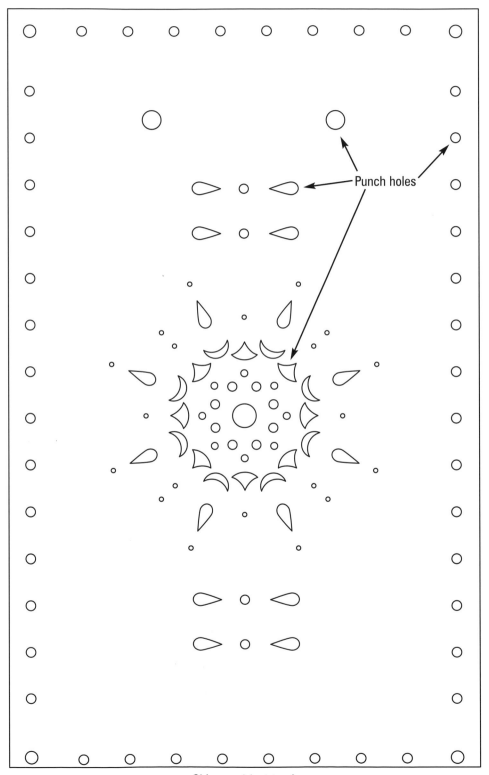

Punch holes

Side panel (cut two)

No enlarging needed

Punch holes

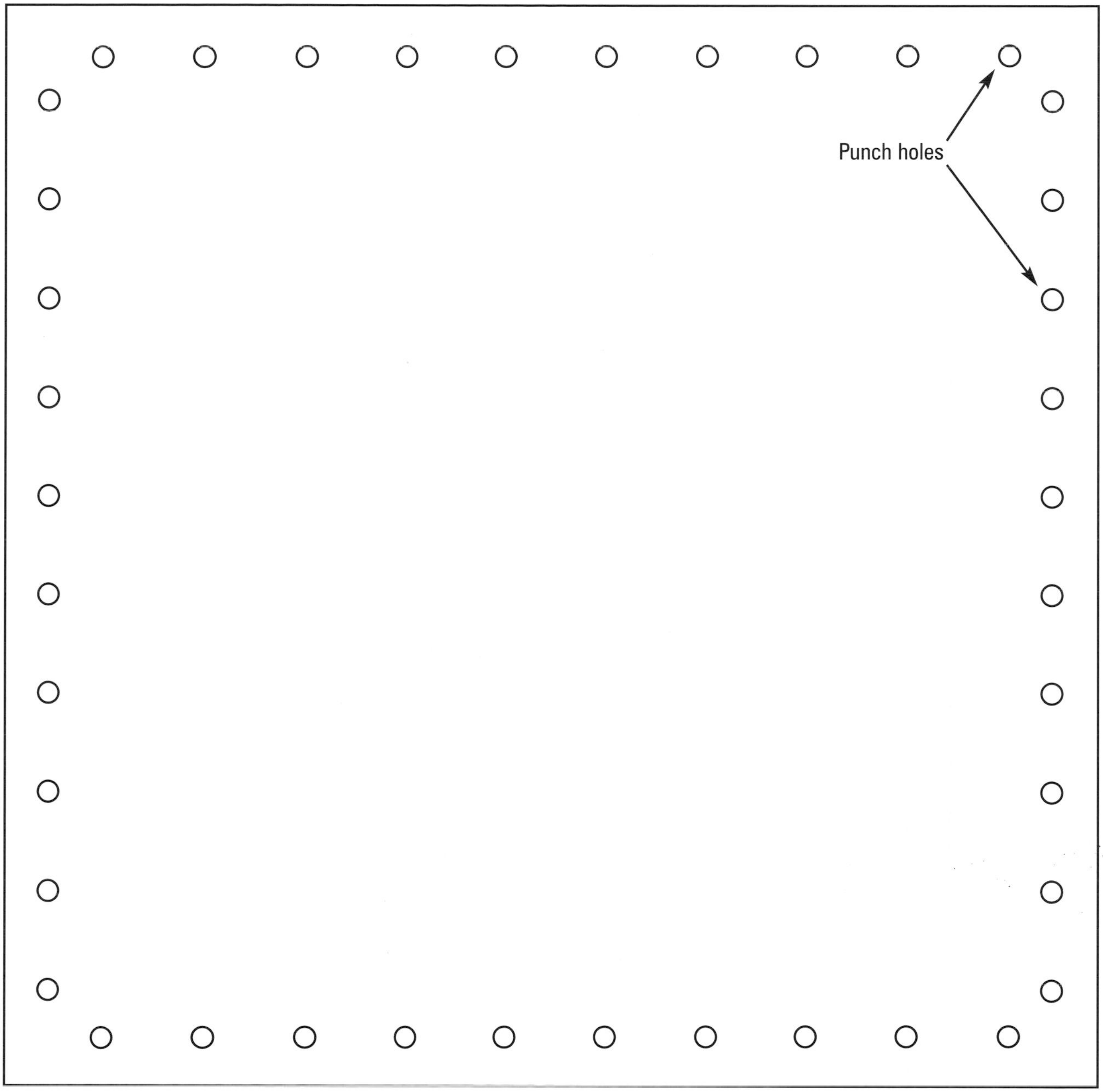

Base (cut two)

Acknowledgments

• Thanks to The Leather Factory—a company that has supported me in all of my creative endeavors and helped make this book possible by donations of supplies and materials. More specifically, thanks to the members of the company who willingly answered technical questions and helped me throughout the process: My key supporter, Doug Thompson, allowed me to take time away from my everyday duties to develop the projects in this book. Tony and Kay Laier provided valuable information and helped to clarify the tool terminology. Jim Koerber was always accessible and happy to provide answers.

• Thanks to the many supportive companies for information and donations of their products: Blue Moon (beads and beading threads), Chartpak (rub-on metallic transfers), Coats and Clark (thread), Conso (grommet setter), Delta Technical Coatings (acrylic and stencil paint), Gutermann (thread), Fiskars (rotary cutter, shears, and self-healing cutting mat), Golden Artist Colors, Inc. (flow releaser), Jamestown Distributors (eye screws), Jacquard Products (acrylic paint and craft syringes), JBH International, Inc. (buttons), Lazertran Limited (photo transfer), Loew-Cornell (paint brushes and stencil brushes), Magenta (rubber stamps), Pfaff (sewing machines), PSX (rubber stamps), Royal Design Studio (stencils), TransferMagic.com (photo transfers), The Lamp Shop (lamp shade frames), The Uptown Design Company (rubber stamps), Tsukineko (stamp pads and fabric markers), Walnut Hollow (wooden tray), and Zocalo (custom wood stool).

• Thanks to my loving husband and best friend, Johnny Lee, whose love and patience continue to support me in all of my creative efforts. And, to my daughter Tiffani and son Trey for their love and encouragement during the process, even when dinner wasn't on the table!

• Thanks to my mother and father for their love and support. They helped in many ways during the process of creating the book, including playing with my three-year-old son. (I am not sure who appreciated their help more... me, or my son, who was allowed to play in the mud and run around the yard for hours!)

• Thanks to both of my sisters-in-law, Mary Beth and Becky, for allowing me to use the photos of their children for the set of photo transfer pillows. (I can't look at those photos without smiling!)

• Thanks to my mother- and father-in-law, Ellen and Alf, for their generous time and continued desire to help.

• Thanks to Betty Auth, a dear friend and a wonderful designer who introduced me to my editor Katherine Aimone.

• Thanks to my editor Katherine Aimone, who I got to know well during the many months of working together as we edited the book and clarified instructions and technical details. I have great respect and admiration for her as a writer and as a person.

• Thanks to Art Director Tom Metcalf and the photography team of Keith and Wendy Wright for the application of their considerable skill. I enjoyed seeing the beauty of leather through their eyes.

About the Author

Kari Lee has been working as a designer in the craft industry for 20 years and has developed a primary interest in creating and marketing pieces made with leather, suede, and rawhide. Besides working as a key project designer for The Leather Factory (a distributor of premium leather and supplies), Kari has also created projects that have been featured in magazines such as *Craft* and *Needlework Age*, *Crafts*, *Arts and Crafts Magazine*, *The Leather Crafters and Saddlers Journal*, and *Better Homes and Gardens Creative Home*.

Her work has been featured in books such as *Stamping with Style* (Lark Books, 2001), and *The Guide to Decorative Stamping* (Watson-Guptill, 1998). She has made guest appearances on various television programs, including HGTV's *Carol Duvall Show* and the Discovery Channel's *Home Matters*. Kari resides in Texas, with her husband and two children.

A Note About Suppliers

Usually, the supplies you need for making the projects in Lark books can be found at your local craft supply store, discount mart, home improvement center, or retail shop relevant to the topic of the book. Occasionally, however, you may need to buy materials or tools from specialty suppliers. For this book the author has provided specific names of suppliers that you can access via the internet. Visit us at www.larkbooks.com, click on "Craft Supply Sources," and then click on the topic.

Index